Nine Out Of Ten

THE LAMBOURN PRESS

Her Majesty The Queen Mother presenting prizes to Mr. F. T. Winter and myself after Plundering's win in the 1986 Whitbread.

Nine Out Of Ten

An autobiography
by
Simon Sherwood

THE LAMBOURN PRESS
London · Dublin · Melbourne

THE LAMBOURN PRESS LTD
The Old Forge, 7 Caledonian Road,
London, N1 9DX, England
28 Molesworth Street, Dublin 2, Eire
9 Queen Street, Melbourne 3000, Victoria, Australia

First published 1989

ISBN 0-9513697-7-6
Published simultaneously with the trade hardback Edition is
Limited and Specially Bound Edition in
Quarter Leather Limited to 175 copies (ISBN 0-9513697-8-4)
by
The Marlborough Bookshop and Sporting Gallery
6 Kingsbury Street, Marlborough, Wiltshire

Jacket design by Peter Hedges
Book from a design by Rupert Collens and Peter Fitzmaurice

Foreword

It is said that a week in politics is a long time, and according to Fred Winter, for whom I rode for fifteen years, racing is much the same. I can remember telling him, one Sunday in November, 1985, that I would be retiring at the end of that season, and I equally well remember him shaking his head and going to great lengths to explain how it would be a very long time before he would be able to find a replacement. The very long time turned out to be six days, the someone Simon Sherwood.

Simon never actually took up the job with Fred Winter because he'd already begun riding for his brother Oliver but, as usual, the Guv'nor had been right and it was on one of his horses, Glyde Court, that I remember first thinking that Simon had something special that set him aside from nearly all of the other jockeys. He was still an amateur at the time but, even at that stage of his career, he had the rare ability to make everything look easy, and to always be one thought ahead of everyone else. Almost more important, he appeared to be totally as one with whichever horse he was riding. His performance on Desert Orchid in the '89 Gold Cup was as good as any I've seen from a National Hunt Jockey, and typical of what one had come to expect from him. When he chose to retire, at the end of the 1988/89 season, jumping lost one of its major exponents.

Fortunately for racing, he isn't leaving the game altogether but, just getting a transfer to the other side and is following his brother into the training ranks. If he shows the same intelligence and determination there as he did when he was riding, then Oliver had better watch out.

Acknowledgements

I, Simon Sherwood, would like to thank my family, friends and racing colleagues for jogging my memory and lending me 'snaps'. I also express my thanks to Bruce Urquhart for helping with early drafts of the book.

I would like to join with the Publishers in thanking Clive Bettison, Lambourn's historian, Terry Selby of *Point to Pointers and Hunter Chasers,* Tim Cox who helped with facts and figures and all the press photographers who rallied round and supplied photographs so quickly.

Picture Acknowledgements

The Publishers would like to thank the following photographers for allowing them to reproduce their photographs in this book: Iain Banks, Gerry Cranham, John Crofts, Fotosport, Fotosport Racing, Kit Houghton, Bernard Parkin, The Press Association, 'Seagram', Colin Turner, Fiona Vigors, Alan Wright and any others not listed.

Contents

The King George VI Chase 1986
December 1986

The King George VI Chase, due to be run at Kempton Park on Boxing Day, 1986, was certainly not to the forefront of my mind as I sat down to breakfast on 17th December in my brother Oliver's house at Lambourn. To be truthful it wasn't on my mind at all as I hadn't a ride in the race and was unlikely to be offered one.

It was, as they say, one of those days. One of my riding-out boots had a hole in it and when we pulled out for the first lot I walked into a puddle. I got a wet foot which soon became a nasty, wet, very cold foot on the gallops. We schooled the first lot, which was not a great success, probably due to my leaking boot and, as a result, Oliver was in a filthy mood as we sat down for breakfast. If all that wasn't enough, the reality of having to go out and buy Christmas presents had just dawned on me; what was I going to get and when was I going to buy them?

It was no surprise that when Chris Hill, David Elsworth's long-standing secretary, rang me he was greeted with the normal gruff 'hello?'. My manner soon changed when he told me his guv'nor wanted a word with me and I sat up very quickly.

David Elsworth, by late 1986, was already established as one of the leading trainers in the South of England, both of jumpers and flat race horses, and any jockey was more than pleased to get a call which could result in rides for his powerful stable.

'Simon, I've got two horses in the King George, Combs Ditch and Desert Orchid,' he said. 'I expect you know a bit about them, are you free for one of them?'

The answer was an emphatic 'Yes'.

I knew I was going to Kempton on Boxing Day but had nothing to ride in the feature race of the day, the King George VI Chase. It is arguably the second most prestigious steeplechase, after the Cheltenham Gold Cup, and therefore attracts the very best staying chasers in training, many of whom clash again in March at the National Hunt Festival in the Gold Cup itself.

Being 'in the right place at the right time' is an expression you hear all too often, but it is probably more true in racing than anywhere else. The success of an individual in racing doesn't always depend on being the best qualified or most experienced for the job and often rests on grabbing opportunities 'when and if' and making the most of them. That call from David Elsworth was one of those opportunities in my case.

The National Hunt season of 1986/1987 had been going quite well up until Christmas, although being attached to Oliver's yard, whose horses consisted primarily of novice hurdlers and chasers, I lacked the back up of a top horse to compete in Grade One races. When the fateful call from

Dessie and I with a circuit to go to win the 1986 King George VI Chase.

David Elsworth came on 17th December I had already ridden twenty-eight winners and was fifth in the Jockey's list.

I then had a week or so to worry about which horse I was going to end up on at Kempton. Colin Brown, David Elsworth's regular jockey and a close friend of mine, was not going to commit himself until he had to, although in a way I was hoping he might side for the grey, Desert Orchid.

I only knew the same as everyone else about the grey horse; he went very fast for two or two-and-a-half miles, was a spectacular, if not reckless, jumper and as a young horse had the reputation of being something of a tear-away. In fact, it would be fair to say that all in all he looked a pretty dangerous ride. The chestnut, Combs Ditch, on the other hand, appeared a far more appealing prospect. He had been second in the great race twice before and was a reliable jumper.

In the period between the fateful call and Boxing Day I had three more wins; one on 19th December at Fakenham and a useful double on the last day of racing before Christmas - 22nd December - at Towcester; so I was in form.

On Boxing Day as I left Lambourn to drive the forty odd miles to Kempton, I still had no idea what I was riding. I left two hours earlier than I normally would, using the potential traffic as an excuse, but in reality it was a terrible feeling of the unknown mixed with excitement and anticipation that made me get my wheels going so early.

The sight of Colin Brown in the weighing room did nothing to relieve my anxiety about which horse I was to ride - still no decision. Colin had walked the course and checked the ground.

Half an inch of rain had fallen on Christmas Day, but it hadn't altered the ground sufficiently to influence Colin's decision.

On such occasions one loves someone else to take the decision. It saves the agony of making it oneself and, more importantly, there is someone else to blame if it is the wrong decision!

The racing papers were full of Combs Ditch at 4 to 1, second favourite to Forgive'n Forget, a 2 to 1 shot who was certainly strongly fancied by many of the leading journalists.

Desert Orchid was 16 to 1, sixth favourite in a field of nine runners and, sure enough, after a quick visit to the canteen, I came back to find the blue and grey colours, with grey cap, hanging on my peg in the changing room. Colin had chosen Combs Ditch, so I was riding Desert Orchid. My immediate thoughts were: will I get run away with and will I end up on the Sunbury turf?

Luckily I had a couple of rides in two races before the big one - finishing third in both. At least that kept my mind off my appointment with Desert Orchid - three hours sitting in the changing room brooding would not have been good for the nerves.

Colin gave me a quick briefing. All I needed to hear at this stage was that Desert Orchid took a grip to the start. I generally feel it is better to know absolutely nothing about a horse before you ride it, judging it on your own instincts rather than knowing a bit. As they say, 'a little knowledge can be a dangerous thing'.

As I entered the paddock, David Elsworth pulled me aside before I was surrounded by the Burridge clan. He summed up his two runners very briefly, describing Combs Ditch as the steady card and Desert Orchid, who was unproven over three miles or more, as the wild card. He felt that if the grey stayed then he would win and my only instructions were to pop Desert Orchid out and give him a chance.

Colin was right. Cantering to the start I had to use Peter Scudamore on Bolands Cross as a crash barrier to stop us, otherwise Desert Orchid and myself may well have jumped the first fence before the start! We inspected the first fence, walked back behind the tape, girths were checked, the tape came down and a moment later we were off. As instructed I popped Desert Orchid out quickly from the gate and Richard Rowe, in Jim Joel's famous black and red colours on Door Latch, jumped off with me, but with Desert Orchid eating up his fences, we were soon out in front on our own. To my surprise he didn't pull. In fact he was very relaxed and far from being reckless at his obstacles, he jumped fast and accurately.

I tried to set an even gallop in front giving Desert Orchid a breather turning into the straight for the first time and then, as we came to the second last on the far side for the second time, I decided to quicken the tempo. The response was such that I felt for the first time in the race we could win.

In any National Hunt race, when you are in front and have decided you are in a winning position, the final bend turning into the straight seems to go on for ever and ever. This dreadful feeling was worsened on that occasion as never before had I had a real chance of winning a race of the importance of the King George. It was further intensified by the fact that the race was over three miles and Desert Orchid had never raced further than two-and-a-half miles. I allowed myself one glance behind, only to see the yellow colours of Forgive'n Forget getting ever closer under Mark Dwyre's distinctive rowing style of driving.

I didn't want to ask Desert Orchid too much at the first fence in the straight - the third last - as we still had over two furlongs left and the longer I could keep him on the bridle the better. The second last fence sealed the fate of my pursuers, another brilliant jump took us a further three lengths clear and it was a case of popping the last to come home fifteen lengths clear of Door Latch.

The reception coming back to the winners' enclosure was unbelievable, in fact outrageous in the best possible way. The roar from the crowd was something I had never experienced before. The euphoria while unsaddling was unparalleled. The only seemingly relaxed character of us all was Desert Orchid.

It was of course as big a day for the Burridge clan as it was for me. None of us had ever experienced such success before and little did we realise in those few mad moments after the race that we were going to scale even greater heights.

But I did not have long to savour these mad moments as I had a ride in the next race for my old guv'nor, Gavin Pritchard-Gordon, and won that also, by the same margin, fifteen lengths.

Colin Brown, as one would expect from one of the most popular men in the changing room, was fulsome in his congratulations. On my way home, I called into one of my regular watering holes, The Swan at Great Shefford, to meet up with Oliver, Steve Smith-Eccles and some other jockeys. In walked a figure with a beard, glasses and wearing a 'dirty flasher's mac'. He ordered a pint and it was only when he had been served that we realised it was Colin in disguise. He didn't want to be recognised! Few of us could have taken picking the wrong horse in the King George VI in the spirit that Colin did.

Me aged about one.

Oliver aged about four.

Childhood and School Days

March 1958 - July 1976

My very earliest memories are, at best, slightly confused on account of living on either side of the country. When I was a year old my parents split up - father remained in Essex, while mother moved to Warwickshire. I was born in a Colchester hospital on the 19th March 1958, and christened Simon Edward Harlakenden Sherwood.

Soon after parting from my mother, father got married again, to Diana, and a couple of years after my arrival they had a son, David, my half-brother.

Easthorpe Hall, where my father lives, was obviously named in the past by someone with delusions of grandeur, for the house certainly wouldn't fit most people's idea of a hall. It is, in fact, nothing more than a sensible Essex country house in what they call 'Suffolk pink'. It would easily qualify for that estate agents' description, 'warm and friendly with seven bedrooms'.

The farm, on the other hand, is very much in keeping with 'hall' status - over 2000 acres which have been built up during the post-war years. My father, Nat, inherited a 1000-acre farm which had originally been bought by his father who, although he had been a 'City man', had plenty of dealings with seed-merchants and clearly felt both the need and the opportunities were right to buy a farm which, even in those days, was not considered large by Essex standards.

Father took it on following a fairly inactive war due to a heart condition. He was, however, a young man fired with plenty of enthusiasm, an entrepreneurial spirit and the foresight to realise that post-war land prices would be such that land had to be bought.

This cavalier spirit was frowned upon by many people in Essex, and as he bought another 200 or 300 acres they would often say, 'That Nat Sherwood must be mad buying land for £120 an acre'. But father is a pretty determined person and perhaps his determination even makes him bigoted at times. Certainly he is not easily dissuaded and carried on, regardless of public opinion, eventually to increase the farm to its present size. In retrospect his critics have been made to look rather stupid.

The farm, as you might expect from the aggressive buying policy, is a 'go-ahead concern', nowadays run more by the farm manager than by father who would be best described as 'out to enjoy life to the full' and he still has the most fantastic twinkle in his eye. But when he gets angry, he gets very angry and very argumentative, something which both my elder brother Oliver and I have certainly inherited.

My father's philosophy, which he practised from an early age, is 'never go to the grave wishing you had when you hadn't'. He used to adore his hunting. At school he was one of the founders of the Radley College Beagles, when at university was Master of the Cambridge Draghounds and then became Master of the local pack of foxhounds, the East Essex. When Oliver and myself were in our teens, we used to take his horses and our ponies down to the West Country, so we could all go hunting with the Devon and Somerset Staghounds.

Father was a keen point-to-point rider, riding over fifty winners on his mainly home-bred horses, and his farm in Essex includes the land on which the Marks Tey point-to-point course is situated.

If my father is argumentative then my mother, Heather (who re-married and is now called Motion) is a member of the 'never wrong, sometimes mistaken' coterie, and combines this with a dogged determination to get her own way. She is also a confirmed addict of hunting, spending most of her time hunting in Warwickshire. She is a wonderful horsewoman with a great eye for a horse and has few peers when it comes to hunting. Although mother is very much aware of what is going on around her, she normally prefers to relax at home in the evenings, and put her feet up, rather than going out to cocktail or dinner parties.

My earliest memories of Essex are, oddly, of my grandmother's house about four miles from the family house. Prested Hall is a large country house in about fifty acres of parkland and my grandmother lived there alone with Alice, her help around the house. Maybe it was boredom, or maybe grandmother really enjoyed seeing her grandchildren, but

Me and Oxo at Shipston-on-Stour.

all I can remember, when I was about four, was Oliver and myself going for tea three or four times a week. Alice was a star and would spoil us rotten with fantastic scones and strawberry jam. But tea was more than just scones and jam. The house had a lovely old-fashioned swimming pool which we played in, there was also a wooden train in which we pedalled around the lawn and various trees for make-believe games.

Mind you, I was always the under-dog. I'm not entirely sure when I realised I had an elder brother. Oliver was no doubt keen to impress upon me at the earliest opportunity the importance of his existence and, equally important, that he was three years older. Whether I accepted this fact or not, I cannot remember, but we would certainly fight 'cat and dog' and I was rarely, if ever, in the position to come out the victor. Things were certainly not improved when someone gave both of us boxing gloves for a present. We spent our whole time re-enacting Frazier-v-Mohammed Ali, which was all well and good until a loose punch hit one of us and then we were off. There was no more acting, it was war.

Our birthdays are within four days of each other. When I was three or four, we were both given pedal cars for our birthdays. The trouble was that Oliver's was a jeep with headlights that didn't work, while mine was a police car with headlights that did work. I am the first to admit that I haven't got a very good temper but Oliver's is terrible. We were at mother's house in Shipston-on-Stour. Oliver was so enraged he hid in the yard, in his jeep, waiting for me in my police car with its lovely working headlights. Then when I appeared, he pedalled straight at me, absolutely flat out, and ran head-on into me smashing my lights. He was much happier.

Until I went to prep school, most of my time was spent with my mother and after that holidays were equally divided between Essex and Warwickshire. Father married Diana, who had been married to my step-father Robert Motion. Diana is a very warm and understanding person who loves the company of the young. Mother had married Rob, Diana's ex-husband, a farmer and one of the most charming men you could ever wish to meet. Tall and distinguished, modest and a true countryman, he is a dedicated hunting man, and until 1988 worked full-time on his 300-acre farm. It was inevitable that with at least ten horses on the 300-acre farm at any one time, I was going to be taught the finer points of horse-manship at an early age!!

There wasn't an instant passion for riding, mother had to bribe both Oliver and myself. There was a farm at Whatcote, a couple of miles away, which made very good ice-cream. We were promised that if we rode there we could have an ice-cream so off we would go, mother either leading me on foot or from a bicycle.

I started competing when I was five in 'leading rein classes'. Mother was always fiercely competitive and the first indication that I had inherited some of that competitiveness started to show through. I was quick to appreciate that success depended, not on the speed of the pony, but the handler. Shouting at or hitting the pony would get one nowhere, so instead I shouted at and hit mother-something which probably accounted for her premature retirement as my 'leading-rein handler', handing over her duties to Oliver.

The two of us gelled well to form a very successful team - Oliver had the cunning of leading rein classes still fresh in his mind and with the team coach, mother, watching from the side-lines, we were able to use a number of well thought out tricks to our advantage.

Alice was a star

Horsemanship from an early age was natural in our family.

However, it was a year later when I was given a pony called Coffee that I really tasted proper success, with no one leading me, for the first time. There can be no denying that Oliver and myself were extremely lucky with our ponies. They were in a word 'superb' - not because they were bought expensively with proven records, but because mother was so good at schooling both them and us.

Coffee taught me the art of show-jumping and in no time we were winning any and every class. That lasted for a couple of years and then I moved on to Simon, yet another brilliant pony. I was now about eight-years old and taking this sort of thing very seriously.

I was an avid watcher of show-jumping on television and decided that Harvey Smith was the man to model myself on if I was ever going to get anywhere. He was the most marvellous rider in jump-offs, he always looked cool and unhurried, but was always much the quickest.

In my first ever competition on Simon, I sat pensively waiting in the collecting ring for my turn in a jump-off. Mother had the most marvellous help-cum-nanny, called Thelma who, recognising the seriousness of the situation asked, 'What do you think about just before you go into the ring?'. With a dead-pan face I answered, 'I am Harvey Smith and England depends on me'. It was probably a shade arrogant of me to consider myself as Harvey Smith but, as an eight-year-old, I was enjoying untold success and any possibility of not finishing in the frame was unthinkable.

With the arrival of Kittywake, a grey Connemara Pony, my attentions turned to eventing. By now, things were becoming more professional. If I was going to win, Kittywake had to be brilliant at all three disciplines - dressage, show-jumping and cross-country. You could not have found a better cross-country pony and show-jumping was fine as well, but the dressage, no doubt due to my inabilities, was somewhat unpolished.

So, for two weeks before I came back on holiday, Kittywake would go off.for a brush-up course to Katie Crilley, who is a professional dressage and event trainer. It did the trick. We were either placed or in the top ten of most of the Pony Club one-day events we took part in.

While my career as an event rider (or so I thought) was gradually taking shape, I was managing to pursue a more conventional education. Life in the classroom started at Mr.Cross's, a fine pre-prep school catering for no more than fifteen pupils, all destined for great scholastic careers, except for me and, possibly, my 'best friend' Percy Sewell.

As I had left by the time I was aged eight-and-a-half, I only have

Coffee and I pretending we are jumping for England.

vague memories, the best being the dripping sandwiches and milk we had at 'elevenses' and the worst being one of my first really painful experiences, which I expand on below.

After school, Percy and I were always collected together and he would come home to mother's to do his homework. Someone deemed it unwise to allow the two of us to work in the same room, the feeling being that it would do little to enhance our academic careers. However, we found plenty of opportunities to discuss matters of great importance to us, not least how to avoid doing our homework. One day we came up with a real 'cracker' - we had to copy from a book, finishing at an asterisk which had been pencilled in. The simplest plans are always the best and this couldn't have been simpler; rub out the asterisk and move it up the page. What we failed to appreciate was the imprint left by the original asterisk; our devious plan resulted in five very painful raps around the knuckles.

Mr. Cross did what was expected of him and in the beginning of the summer term 1966, I was off to join my brother as a boarder at Wellesley

House, Broadstairs, on the Kent coast. The school had been for a long time one of the leading prep schools in the country, especially good at producing top-class games players. During my entire school career I achieved more at Wellesley than anywhere else. Mind you, I got off to a pretty inauspicious start as with an older brother there, I was obviously very cheeky and became known as nothing more than a 'right cheeky little brat' and quickly learned to pay for it by being beaten with the slipper.

I don't know what it is, but at some stage during prep school one gets an attack of the 'Steve McQueens and the Great Escape'. Fortunately two friends were suffering from the same problem at the same time. There was nothing to do but escape. The exact destination seemed unimportant - London, a few safe houses, even France was mooted, but that was all some way off. No, the object of the whole operation was to get out of school so, with that in mind, the plans were laid.

Boiler suits were the order of dress, heavily weighed down with provisions, mainly oranges and bananas and as much money as we could

Wellesley House uniform. I am not looking as much of a scarecrow as usual.

muster (about sixpence each) plus torches. I peaked too early. Running out of 'Steve McQueen and the Great Escape' pills at the top of the stairs, the wish to escape had totally deserted me and on occasions like that there is nothing else to do but go back to bed. My companions were undeterred by this early setback, setting off on phase one - getting down the stairs. Disaster struck immediately. A torch unfortunately bounced its way down sixty stairs. So much for France. They didn't even get to the bottom of the stairs, while in the meantime, I was well tucked up in bed.

Mentioning bananas reminds me of quite a funny story as, at about this time, they were my staple diet at home. One day mother, Oliver and myself took about a dozen of them to a horse show, but, to everyone else's annoyance, no one could find them when we got there. After searching high and low, it was decided that the bananas must have been left at home. In the meantime, I kept very quiet and would have got away with it had Oliver not got out of the Land Rover as we were leaving to pick up a bucket which had been left behind. There, for all to see, were the skins of a dozen bananas!

I am certain that this is not the right time or place to go into the rights and wrongs of sending children aged eight or nine years as boarders to prep schools. I coped very nicely because Oliver looked after me for my first year or so. 'Fight like cat and dog at home' we may have done, but we were always ready to unite against any real or imagined threat from third parties. Certainly in my case going to prep school was an eye-opener and I had to fend for myself far more than when living at home with mother and going daily to Mr. Cross's. I became aware of what was going on around me and naturally started to grow up quickly.

I didn't mind going back to school. What I minded was arriving at Victoria Station to catch the school train and standing on the platform surrounded by old wood-wormed and moth-eaten 'hand-me-down' cases and tuck boxes, dating back to my father's days. Things like that mattered a lot and to see all my friends with their smart Billings and Edmonds cases and tuck boxes was about all the indignation I could cope with, although I struck back with a vengeance at the start of one term.

Mother had to go somewhere and therefore couldn't take me to Victoria. My cousin, Jane Hilder, an extremely attractive twenty-five-year-old model, was called in to do the job and when I told everyone she was my sister, I became everyone's best friend for twenty-four hours.

But, if my school baggage had a lot to answer for, my uniform wasn't a great improvement. The uniform at Wellesley was as varied as it was (on occasions) uncomfortable. Knickerbockers, hairy and itchy in the winter term, a tweed suit in the Lent term and a short grey suit and a blazer in summer. Most of these were okay if they fitted you, unfortunately mine didn't. They came from Oliver who was somewhat bigger than me so consequently I spent my whole time walking around looking like a badly dressed scarecrow!

My success at Wellesley was based on, not my indifferent dress nor my supposed sister, but my ability on the games field. I am certainly not a 'natural' but I soon realised I had above average talent at games which I'm glad to say was noticed by the masters. I played in the first teams of all the major sports - rugby for three years, captaining it for one season; I was captain of football for two seasons and was in the cricket team for two seasons, in my last year opening the batting with the Kent and England cricketer Chris Cowdrey.

After five years and one term it was off as a boarder again to join Oliver at public school (Radley). I arrived there at the beginning of the winter term, aged thirteen in 1971. It was perhaps a slightly close run thing as I had to take the Common Entrance Exam twice. It wasn't because I was thick, anyway I like to think I wasn't, but Radley was a very hard school to get into when I was trying.

Radley is on the edge of the River Thames, between Abingdon and Oxford. There is nothing extraordinary about the school; it is a good public school with only about 500 pupils. There are eight houses, known as 'socials', and even if some of us weren't terribly bright, we at least looked it wearing black gowns around school. Although they sound very impractical and rather old-fashioned, they were marvellous in that they kept the rest of our clothes clean.

Old boys prominent in sport include in racing, Brough Scott, the Channel 4 presenter; Gavin Pritchard-Gordon, the Newmarket trainer; his brother Grant, Khaled Abdulla's racing manager; Nicky Vigors, a former trainer and now a starter of The Jockey Club; Kim Bailey, the trainer who bought Vigors' old yard in Lambourn, and Michael Heaton-Ellis, who works for the Maktoum family and is now confined to a wheelchair after a terrible fall at Huntingdon. Outside racing there is Ted Dexter, chairman of the England cricket selectors.

I arrived in 'A' social and wasted no time establishing myself as a 'nervy stig', Radley's idiom for a cheeky new boy. With a brother three

I opened the batting for Wellesley one year with Chris Cowdrey - he is centre bottom.

years ahead of me in the same social and knowing a number of his friends, I felt like a seasoned campaigner, but was soon brought back to earth in no uncertain manner. Ronnie Rees was, and still is, a small physics teacher who wears glasses and, because of his appearance, pupils endeavoured to get the upper hand. I endeavoured to get the upper hand in my first year. He told me to do something and, thinking he couldn't hear me, I told him to 'bugger off'. He did hear me and threw me out of the class. Nervy stigs like myself objected to being thrown out of class and to show my disapproval I kicked the classroom door which, in retrospect, was a pretty silly thing to do. Mr Rees told me to go to see the Warden. Thinking I had the whole situation under control I decided I would leave that visit out of my list of appointments. Two weeks later the Warden asked me why I hadn't seen him. D.R.W. Silk is an imposing man to meet at the best of times but when you are in your first year at Radley and you have delayed meeting him by a fortnight, he becomes formidable. A double first and a double blue at Cambridge was altogether far too much for me and half-an-hour after going into his study I emerged mentally battered and bruised and very definitely no longer a nervy stig.

On the whole I drifted through Radley; I finished as a house monitor but it would be fair to say I was a bit anti establishment, the sort of person who wore beads around his neck! I got my 'O'levels and two 'A'levels - Oliver only managed one 'A'level and, taking that as the only real guideline to our intelligence, I have always claimed I'm twice as clever as him.

Oliver, on the other hand, was a dedicated sportsman at Radley and it was through dogged perseverance that he won places, albeit occasionally, in the school's first teams. From a sports angle I was a disappointment. Up to Colts standard I played in all the teams but then my dedication slipped and this, combined with my size, led to me gradually fading from the scene.

Unlike most of my contemporaries I stopped growing after prep school and when I was sixteen I only weighed seven stone. Sixteen-year-olds who weigh seven stone and ride have only one future - to become flat jockeys; with that in mind and with the help of Geoffrey Gibbs, the Jockey Club Handicapper, I thought about going to either Sam Armstrong or Ben Hanbury as a flat apprentice. But fate dealt a cruel blow. At the moment critique, i.e. the summer holidays before I expected to go to Newmarket, I grew two inches and put on a stone, killing that idea, much to the relief of my parents.

Two inches might have stopped me becoming the next Lester Piggott but it didn't stop anybody who was in a position to throwing me out of pubs, cinemas and generally anywhere with an age limit. That was not cool and not in keeping with my attempted style. Drastic action had to be taken. It came in the form of a pop newspaper, *Melody Maker*, advertising 'five-inch stacks' - these would totally alter my life. They survived one outing: I found myself having to hide from a master in Oxford and one run down a street was enough for my feet and ankles. To this day they have remained firmly at the back of a cupboard. But as one door closes another opens. My sporting prowess might have abandoned me but I was discovering that there was more to girls than just riding ponies. I bought my first girlfriend, Alice Thorne (niece of the late John Thorne who put up such a heroic performance, aged fifty-four, when finishing second on Spartan Missile in the 1981 Grand National). I was thirteen, she was a year older and we were at Pony Club camp. My tactic was simplicity itself - I went straight up to her (as only a man does when he has such a mission) and offered her a threepenny piece if she became my girlfriend. Such arrogance normally has disastrous consequences but not on this occasion. She accepted and for nearly two years we were the closest of friends, seeing a lot of each other in the holidays but, more importantly, writing to each other while at school, which was always considered very cool!

Warwickshire could not have been a more perfect place to pursue my new found interest. Initially parties were orientated around the Pony Club but, as one got older, more and more people had their own parties which steadily became wilder! By the time I was fifteen every holiday had a pretty full social diary. With the aid of my old friend, Percy Sewell, most of these ended in one drama or another.

The Warwickshire Pony Club had a dance at a hotel in Stratford-upon-Avon and Percy and myself thought it would be amusing to take two girls upstairs for a 'cuddle'. We were only fifteen or so and I can assure you it was to be nothing more than a cuddle. We found our girls and the

Mother at the Moreton-in-the-Marsh Show.

whole thing would have been perfect had we only kept an eye on the time. It suddenly dawned on us that the only parents downstairs waiting were ours. Panic set in, compounded by the fact that the father of one of the girls was Adam Butler M.P.. An instant plan had to be made - the girls would go down the main stairs while Percy and I would go down the fire-escape at the back of the hotel and appear a few minutes later. In our haste I ripped an arm off my dinner jacket, catching it on something down the fire-escape and, not surprisingly, we weren't in Adam Butler's list of top ten friends that night.

As I said earlier, as we got older, the parties got wilder. By now I could drive and had an old Escort with appalling headlights. Three of us were going to a fancy-dress party, Percy dressed as an Arab, someone called Christian Hoyer-Miller as a tart and myself as a punk-rocker. The headlights let us down badly and we crashed. We had nothing to do but ring Major Sewell, Percy's father, who insisted when he collected us that we had to go to Warwick Hospital for a check-up. The embarrassment of

Towards the end of my Pony Club career on my brilliant pony, Kittywake.

walking into the hospital was unparalleled, further heightened when out dropped a condom from Percy's pocket while he was being checked, landing at the Major's feet. The Major quietly bent down and picked up the much carried around item and said, 'Well, you won't be needing that tonight'.

But, I suppose, looking back, the worst moments came at school dances. There is nothing on the school curriculum to compete with school dances. Most boys are up to facing another fifteen overgrown and hairy individuals on a rugby field, but confront them with their counterparts from a girls' school at a school dance, and even the bravest is inclined to wince. However, on the occasion I have in mind, I wasn't engaged in unarmed combat with an opponent from another school but the daughter of a Radley master. It was the Lent term of 1976, everything was going according to plan, all the indications suggested I was on course to ride my first winner and, as they say in racing, 'I turned into the straight with a double-handful'.

Possibly my inability to get into many 'X-rated films' in the past had some bearing on my performance, but for five minutes I worked very hard, achieving very little and thinking there isn't much to all this. Fortunately, experience wasn't a failing of the girl in question and, after a surfeit of over-excitement on my part, she helped me by pulling down her tights!! An important lesson was learned that day.

Tom Goddard with his and my rucksacks.

Me in Capetown (beads were still cool!)

African Travels

August 1976 - May 1977

I left Radley at the end of the summer term 1976. The School encouraged the idea that ex-pupils should broaden their outlook and travel rather than being nepotistic and going straight into a family business. To use a fairly frank Antipodean phrase, they encouraged us to 'Sow our wild oats if possible'

There was a travelling scholarship which had been given by an Old Radleian, John Nugee, specifically designed to help individuals with that very idea in mind. Before leaving Radley, potential candidates submitted their proposals and if they were considered original enough in thought, financial assistance was given.

Tom Goddard was the poor unfortunate who thought it might be fun to travel with me. We were in different socials but had become good friends during the two 'A'level years and had discussed at some length the opportunities open to us through the scholarship. Tom was a very quiet, unassuming individual at school but in South Africa it soon became evident there was supreme confidence behind the quiet exterior. While the noisy ones like myself tried to impress straight away, Tom with his height and good looks would patiently bide his time, eventually walking away with much the prettiest girl.

Both of our brothers had been to Australia - Oliver had spent twelve months 'down under' and while it certainly sounded very appealing we felt it lacked originality so we opted for a couple of alternatives, Canada or South Africa. Canada seemed full of pitfalls - it was virtually impossible to get a work permit and if one did manage to get one, there was the problem of the weather and ensuring one didn't catch the worst of the bitterly cold climate. So South Africa, from a simple process of elimination, became the choice, improved by the fact we were put onto a firm which specialised in sending students to South Africa, finding them work and, of course, work permits. The best jobs on offer were as travelling salesmen for Multitude, a firm which sold pens and rubber stamps. By accepting the jobs while still in England, we were granted work permits for an unlimited period in South Africa.

Preparations were brief, we only had three weeks before we flew to Johannesburg and it was really just a case of packing rucksacks with jeans, tee-shirts, trainers and sleeping-bags. We hardly noticed the three weeks passing and before we knew where we were, we had landed in a deserted Johannesburg on a Sunday in August 1976. Johannesburg on a Sunday is not the sort of place at which to arrive when you are not totally au fait with travelling around the world. The Afrikaaners are deeply religious and obviously when we arrived they were mainly in church! Those who weren't should have been to cleanse their souls as they were so unhelpful. However, we eventually found the Y.M.C.A. and I was treated to the delights of Room 827 with a bunk bed and a loo in the corner.

Selling biros and rubber stamps was indeed very different from life at Radley and at times soul destroying. We were split up into three man sales teams all in one car and sent off on a seven day trip to cover a specific number of towns. Each member of the team then struggled to get as much business as possible in their designated area, all meeting for lunch to take a rain check, then working through to about 5.00 p.m.. It was satisfying to re-appear at the end of the day carrying a mass of money but heart-breaking if you had slogged your way up and down every street in your area and ended up with absolutely nothing. We were paid on commission only, so there was considerable pressure on us to sell as many biros and rubber stamps as possible. It is a great way of rewarding good salesmen but I certainly wasn't one, so consequently, not only was my new found employment depressing, at times it was, to put it mildly, very poorly paid into the bargain.

Accommodation on these excursions was somewhat varied, depending largely on who we knew or where we were. Our VW Beetle played mobile home for a large proportion of the time. Whatever charm Beetles might have, comfort is not one of them. The degree of comfort in the three 'sleeping compartments' varied from terrible to atrocious, requiring a strictly adhered to rota. The passenger's seat was very definitely first class accommodation, while the back seat was appallingly claustrophobic and in the driver's seat you were constantly competing with the pedals and the steering wheel. If it wasn't the Beetle it was the ground or the police station for the night.

I could put together an Egon Ronay guide of 'Police Cells in South Africa' as Tom and I must have slept in over twenty-five of them dotted around the country. Tom had the patter off to a T and was responsible for doing the talking. He would explain, at some length, to the officer on duty about our impoverished state, that we were students travelling, had nowhere to stay and wondered if he might offer us any encouragement. All being well a white cell would be free (they tended to have fewer occupants than their black equivalents!). This form of accommodation was perfectly acceptable as long as the black cells weren't busy all night. If they were the chances of sleeping were minimal, due the continual drone of African singing. The problem was certainly worsened by the many and varied renditions of favourite songs, seemingly to ensure the harmonic qualities of the station were put to their ultimate test. Breakfast at 5.30 a.m. was a welcome relief, normally just porridge or cereal, but in some of the smarter stations there might be the added bonus of toast, and then it was back to biros and rubber stamps.

Biros and rubber stamps quickly lost their appeal. It was time to find an alternative form of employment. However, due to the South Africans' whole-hearted dislike of being travelling salesmen these were the only jobs available. Next we tried selling 'child education courses'. This was a two-phase job - see the wife in the daytime, convince her how good our product was and, at the same time, book an appointment with her husband in the evening after he returned from work. It quickly became evident why this was such an easy job to get as it was fraught with dangers from the outset. Tom was pounced on by some frustrated wife, who thought Christmas had come early when this tall Englishman appeared at her door; while I was constantly being confronted by signs saying 'ich nie honde' which translated means 'beware of the dog'. The wife was only the start of our problems. Having fought off nymphomaniacs, mad dogs and persuaded the wives this was the perfect product for their child, we then had to return to face over-tired husbands who had no interest in our courses whatsoever. Further, some would look at us with the deepest suspicion, obviously suspecting their wives' daytime motives in showing interest in us and then one could be ordered out of the house in the most alarming manner. Six months working as a travelling salesman was six months too long and the time came to move on, to Cape Town.

Cape Town is, in my view, the prettiest city I have ever been to, a view shared by many people who have visited it. It offers everything - culture, weather, beaches, restaurants and beauty. Tom and I, for once, were able to appreciate some comfort during our stay there. Nigel Odling, a friend from school, lived there with his parents in the very smart suburb of Kenilworth. They welcomed us with open arms and invited us to stay for as long as we wanted, and taking every letter to be the law, we did exactly that. We stayed for a month.

What was all the more astounding was the fact that the Odlings went away after three days leaving us not only the house but also an open top Mercedes sports car to get about in. We certainly lived life to the full, devoting plenty of time to cruising up and down Clifton beach (the beach where anybody who was anybody went!) in our newly found motorised splendour.

All good things have to come to an end and at the end of a month it was back to hitching, up to the Garden Route, then on to Durban, finishing up at the 'concrete jungle' Johannesburg en route to Rhodesia.

Our visit to Rhodesia was badly timed - they were having a war! We were aware there was a war going on, we had read about it in the papers but it never occurred to us we could or would in any way get involved. We drifted on, in a sublime dream that the war would carry on in one part of the country while we were in another!

The picture we drew could not have been more wrong - we were certainly labouring under major delusions until we arrived at the border town of Beitbridge. Here we quickly came back to earth with a nasty bump. At the armed checkpoint we were subjected to severe questioning as to the purpose of our visit which left us in no doubt about the uneasy climate prevailing in Rhodesia. The checkpoint was heavily guarded by forty or so soldiers with rifles and machine-guns who were alert and clearly very much on edge. That was a bad enough shock in itself, but nothing to compare with the shock of seeing the people who were giving us a lift getting three guns out of the boot of the car. The Williams' didn't look the types to have guns in their boot. They were in their fifties and on their way back from seeing a sister in Durban, pretty harmless stuff but oh no, Mr. Williams checked the guns were in good working order and then handed one to Tom and told him to keep it sticking out of the window.

Rhodesia *Kenya*

Well, if I jibbed at the last moment escaping from prep school, you can imagine how I felt now. All I wanted to do was get out of the car and get back to Jo'burg 'a.s.a.p.'. I overcame my nerves, fortunately, because our dramas in Rhodesia were far from over. With a step-mother who had lived in Rhodesia we had a mass of contacts and spent three months just travelling around from one stop to the next. All our contacts were extremely friendly and we had a marvellous time, that is except for the travelling. Rarely did I feel comfortable. Indeed I felt particularly uncomfortable when we were being shot at! Tom and I were in a convoy of about twenty cars, travelling from Bulawayo to Fort Victoria with army jeeps front and rear, both with large machine-guns mounted. The shooting happened very quickly - all I can remember was ducking, thinking that if we weren't killed then we would be caught and tortured! So much for my rather morose imagination. The army soon dealt with the two terrorists and no one in the convoy was hurt.

We ended our African trip meeting my father at Nairobi in Kenya. He had gone to stay with his sister, my Aunt Sybil, who lived just two miles from the capital in a tiny village called Karen. Sybil is a wonderful lady, slightly rotund and very colonial in appearance, wearing khaki, speaking Swahili and enjoying life to the full but tempers the slightly domineering colonial spirit with a very kind and thoughtful nature.

We spent the final three weeks in Kenya at a marvellous place, Ocean Sports, by the sea, which was very much a British haunt and it was not uncommon to run into people one knew. Father learned (which is rare for him) about a side of life he had never come across before. Lying beside the swimming pool reading a book he spotted two very pretty English girls, also lying by the pool, having had a swim and smoking a home-made cigarette, only every time they had a puff, to quote father, 'it seemed to send them', (where I don't know). He was mesmerised by the whole event and promptly went off to buy some cigarettes for the evening, (something he never does being a confirmed pipe smoker), hoping for the same effects. Sadly for father nothing happened, the intricacies of smoking marijuana had eluded him.

Our visit to Kenya was brief but excellent. It was a fitting end to an extraordinary period of my life, a period that certainly opened my eyes to many of life's facets that I hadn't seen before and I am unlikely to encompass again. By then it was May 1977, time to go back to England and the harsh reality of having to knuckle down to some serious and hard work.

Cirencester and Point-to-Pointing
June 1977 - August 1981

I was due to go to Cirencester in September 1977 and by rights was supposed to do a year's practical agricultural labouring. Instead it had to be crammed into four months, starting off with two months at Lord Rayleigh's dairy near Chelmsford. There are few better dairies in the country - large, efficient and productive. It taught me one thing - never be a dairy farmer. After the joys of Africa, getting up at 4.30 a.m. every morning to milk by 6.00 a.m. was not for me.

Thankfully, with those two months out of the way, I went to my godfather, Anthony Round, for another two months practical. He is known to the younger members of our family as 'Uncle Todd'. He is a wonderful godfather but not an easy man. Tall, distinguished and in his sixties, he can be very self-opinionated and purposely ignorant at times. He is the type of person you would love to hate, and by rights probably should, but his magnetic personality draws you closer to him.

He always followed the same routine every morning. At 6.58 a.m. precisely he would walk into the yard, wearing hob-nailed boots and shouting at his black labrador, Teal, punctuated by the odd cough brought on by too much smoking. As a general farm-hand the thought of arriving late filled me with horror. Inevitably it happened and, in a moment of uncontrollable panic, I decided to make up a story. The time between waking late and having to confront your boss and explain why you are late is fairly unpleasant when you are a 'mud student' like me and your boss a man like Anthony Round. In this case my mind became overactive, with various thoughts flashing through it of wild ideas of how to appease him. Uncle Todd's farm was just down the road from father's and passing a few horses in a field, I came up with a marvellous excuse. I told him father's horses had got out and, luckily for everybody they just happened to be on my route to work but unfortunately it had taken me almost an hour to put them back in the field on my own. Todd let me carry on, the story was not only getting more dramatic, it was getting more convincing by the minute. 'Rubbish boy!', he bellowed back, a comment I feared would come. What I stupidly hadn't banked on was him ringing up home and discovering that I'd simply overslept. There was nothing else to do but beat a hasty retreat and try and do a decent day's work.

Farm students, often known as 'mud students', are renowned for being cheap farm labour but they are more famous for making monumental blunders with machinery, nullifying the initial saving on wages. Aware that my day's work was going to be closely scrutinized, I went off with George Ponsonby, a great friend and another embryo Cirencester student, who was also working on the farm, to clean out some stables with a tractor and bucket.

Initially I was razor sharp but it didn't take long for the effects of the morning bollocking to wear off and my concentration wavered as George and I continued our endless discussion on girls and parties. Suddenly, to my horror, I noticed the stable was moving. Without me noticing, the fork-lift on the tractor had lodged itself under the door-frame and picked up the stable, which was now about two feet off the ground. Horror turned to laughter as the two of us thought it was the funniest thing we had ever seen. Without warning George stopped laughing and began to look very uncomfortable; I stupidly never twigged and carried on laughing until I was rudely interrupted by another terrible bellow from behind. Todd had been witness to the whole thing. It was not a good day.

So, in September 1977, I went to Cirencester or, to be more precise, The Royal Agricultural College at Cirencester. I was to spend four very enjoyable years there; firstly I did a two-year farm management course, then another year's practical, which luckily involved quite a bit of time living at home in Essex and riding in point-to-points, followed by a final year back at the college.

I was very fortunate to find a cottage at Cirencester and to be able to share it with two close friends, Henry Eden and James Lambert. The two-year farm management course was comparatively easy, compared to the 'A' level course, and as long as you kept up with your notes, exams were not much of an ordeal. With that in mind, work was a very low priority

Spud bashing on Anthony Round's farm. Henry Eden is the blond boy behind me.

Our cottage near Cirencester - James Lambert in front.

and life at Cirencester revolved around cars (preferably fast), girls and drink (plenty of it), all of which was probably responsible for some friendships which will last for ever and also enabled me to get involved in racing.

In 1979, after two years and a diploma, Henry and I decided to go and work for a large Lincolnshire farmer, Mr. Peter Dennis, to gain some practical experience before returning to Cirencester to do the advanced farm management course. Peter Dennis is a meticulous man, noted for attention to detail and general efficiency and, consequently, is extremely successful, but at the same time exceptionally kind. He and his wife are a most attractive couple - he dresses immaculately and always has his Range Rover cleaned by his chauffeur before he drives around the farm, while his lovely wife, Ann, is great fun.

The Dennis' were very kind to both of us and we learned a lot but somehow we felt rather out on a limb being based up in Lincolnshire. The work allocated to us was wide and varied - anything from sprout picking and spud harvesting to poacher patrol. In September the poachers started to move in and were capable of taking anything up to 200 pheasants in a night. Peter Dennis's shoot was large, in line with everything else on the farm. Naturally it was very well run so, to combat the poachers, patrols were organised up to the first day's shooting.

Henry and I would start at midnight and finish at 7.30 a.m., armed with nothing more than a Land Rover and a thermos. That was until Henry Dennis, our boss's second son, discovered what we were up to which was when the trouble started. Young Dennis was a Falstaff type character - large, warm and quite noisy. He was keen to enjoy life but was going through a divorce at the time and, rather to the detriment of our livers, thought it amusing to come and find us at about 1.00 a.m., armed with a couple of bottles of whisky. We then drank the whisky until we were, to all intents and purposes, unconscious. I don't know what happened to the poachers but we certainly gave the farm manager a fright one morning. He was driving to work only to see the Land Rover parked on the side of the road with the windows open, Henry Dennis's head slumped out of one window, my feet out of the other and Henry Eden lying against my window. Forget the birds, it looked as if the poachers had got us, until the empty evidence was found!

So ended our cushy job as poacher patrolmen and soon we were back on the spud machine. After six or so months of working in Lincolnshire and taking the opportunity to have some of the finest shooting in England, the temptation to return to Essex to pursue my favourite sporting pastime, point-to-pointing, was too great so, come February time, I hot-footed it home.

When I came back from Africa, I had been faced with something of a dilemma - should I carry on eventing or should I give it up? The plan had been to carry on. I had set my sights on eventing and had every intention of trying to get to the top of the three-day event ladder, but I was faced with a couple of glaring complications. Firstly, I didn't have a horse and secondly, I was going to Cirencester.

My entire eventing career had taken place on my brilliant pony, Kittywake, which was fine for the Pony Club, but that was it. We were now confronted with a far greater problem, finding a horse that either was, or had the potential to be, a three-day eventer. At the end of the day they are, to put it mildly, bloody expensive and faced with the prospect of going to Cirencester, which is not really conducive to furthering an eventing career, the idea was scrapped.

Some alternative form of entertainment had to be found and it came in the form of Icy Affaire, a point-to-pointer at home in Essex. He was bred by my father and, in the nicest possible way, was a moderate flat horse, managing to finish third in a bad maiden at Yarmouth when trained by Gavin Pritchard-Gordon. Icy Affaire was, on the other hand, a very good schoolmaster and was responsible for teaching me the basics of race-riding.

Whilst at Cirencester, I had four seasons riding in point-to-points and hunter chases. My first ride in public was at the North Norfolk Harriers Point-to-point on Saturday, 25th March 1978 at Higham. I walked into the paddock hoping for sound advice, not to mention a tactical plan from the trainer, Nat Sherwood. Instead, he told me to go out and enjoy myself.

I might not have known anything about race-riding but I had, in the past, watched Oliver in the paddock at some length and felt I knew how to conduct myself during this period of high visibility. Plenty of practice at home in front of a full length mirror confirmed this fact.

I arrived at the course with time on my hands; I went through all the normal pre-race procedures and I walked the course before going back to the changing tent. Time was dragging, there wasn't enough to do and my body was fast becoming riddled with nerves. The nerves had started to creep into me the day before like a disease, but I was a dedicated point-to-point jockey and couldn't let such things affect me. I hadn't even allowed myself the liberty of a whisky the night before to help me sleep. I had woken up at 5.00 a.m. and thought about nothing else except 'The Race' and there I was sitting in the tent, beginning to wonder how long I was going to be a dedicated jockey.

Eventually the time arrived for me to get changed - wearing my father's old breeches which had been resurrected from the depths of the attic with their buttons below the knee and my new boots, which had been sufficiently treated, with their newly blackened tops, so as not to appear too new. I put on father's green and orange halved colours, gathered up my saddle and accessories and weighed out.

'Come on jockeys!' This was now the moment of truth when I had to leave the tent and make my way to the paddock. I checked that my back protector was still straight, that I did not do my chin strap up too soon and walked nervously, though trying to appear confident to the awaiting entourage in the middle of the paddock. 'Jockeys get mounted!' Having been legged-up, I suddenly felt terribly insecure. When schooling at home you feel confident due to the fact that you have a thick pair of jodhpurs and boots on. However, on the racecourse it was a different matter, the thin boots and breeches offered me no help in staying in the saddle and I wondered whether I would even make it out of the paddock without mishap. Fortunately I did and managed to arrive safely at the start before my next major problem confronted me.

Little did I realise that pulling goggles down could be such a problem. It had always seemed such an easy and effortless job when I'd watched jockeys before the start on the television. I had had my girths checked, we were about to come under orders and there I was struggling, even fighting with the wretched things and getting nowhere fast. Having given up the unequal struggle I was then faced with the ultimate in humiliation - having to ask the starter to hold Icy Affaire while I got both hands on to the job.

By the time the race started I was an exhausted wreck, suffering from shock as we approached the first. Having been used to eventing, hooking up and going 3-2-1 as I came to an obstacle, I was horrified by the speed we were going and I remember thinking to myself 'we can't possibly go so fast'.

After a few fences I began to get more of a feel for this new riding experience but still ended up eighth out of nine finishers. In fact I was lucky to have a ride at all, as racing was abandoned after the fourth race,

In the paddock at Higham before my last ride in my first point-to-point season, 1978 a period of high visibility.

which was won by the local point-to-point hero, David Turner. Next time out things went slightly better and I was third on our home course at Marks Tey.

The Members Race at the East Essex Point-to-point, once again on the home course, on 15th April, was my intended first winner, but I misjudged the greater experience of Charlotte Brew and Barony Fort, who ended up stealing the race from under our nose. As I let her get twenty lengths clear, I think I must have been in some form of mild coma, forgetting the object of the exercise was to catch her and, indeed, pass her. It was a singularly inept piece of riding, not lost on father, who might have omitted to give me any advice before my races, but was certainly not short on post-race criticism. Charlotte and Barony Fort had won their place in the record book the previous season when she was the first girl to ride in the Grand National and was unlucky not to finish the course, pulling up just three fences out.

Icy Affaire and I appeared four times that season and in the final outing I fell off. I got terribly excited coming to the third last at Higham, thinking I might win, and asked him for 'a big one'. He hit the top, came down on his knees and I went straight out of the front door. But I was hooked. I considered myself a fully-fledged jockey and set my sights on winning the Point-to-point Jockeys Championship.

My next encounter with racehorses soon dispelled any notions I might have had about my ability as a jockey. Oliver was now fully ensconced as Fred Winter's assistant, having done a spell with Arthur Moore in Ireland, and with my being just down the road at Cirencester he suggested I came and rode out one morning. It was now September, so I'd been able to enjoy the summer as an aspiring champion jockey and eagerly awaited my morning at Uplands, the famous Lambourn yard of F.T. Winter.

As the morning approached, I became increasingly apprehensive about the whole thing. Oliver had given me strict instructions about what to wear and when to turn up and, having never ridden out for anybody before, the thought of starting at Winter's quickly began to lose its appeal. I arrived on time but got off to a bad start; Fred Winter stood in the yard and watched everyone go past as they were legged-up by either Oliver or Brian Delaney, the head lad. He stood there, looking steely-eyed and pretty fierce. As I got legged-up my saddle slipped back, a crime that shouldn't happen to even the youngest apprentice. As he is a man who doesn't suffer fools gladly, I fully expected him to appear in the box when I was re-tacking the horse, to tell me not to bother and go home. Luckily he didn't.

My chosen mount was something called Silver Steel. Amongst the numerous gallops at Lambourn is a dirt track, about a mile round, which is only really used in August and September, when the ground is too firm to use the grass and horses need to get the mileage in at the beginning of the season. Up to the day I stopped riding it was a gallop I disliked. The plan was to go round three times and, being the newcomer, I was to follow the other six.

The one piece of equipment Oliver left off his list was goggles. When you are seventh out of seven on a dirt gallop, goggles very nearly top the list of essential items. Not by design, but by accident and lack of strength, I overcame the problem in under a circuit - Silver Steel totally took control, pulled his way to the front and took up the running.

I couldn't help but notice the lone, mounted figure sitting, like a Red

Indian scout, on the bank overlooking the gallop, watching all. It was F.T. Winter. I couldn't bear it. I finished exhausted, stiff and I had broken the number one rule on the gallops - do not pass anybody. So, to feel better, I pre-empted my pending ban on the Lambourn gallops by promising myself I'd never, ever do that again, and waited.

Brian Delaney hardly improved the situation. He had been with Fred Winter since the start and was one of the most respected men in Lambourn. When he said something it was gospel and he trotted up to me with a very stern expression and said, 'You have just done the one thing that annoys Mr. Winter more than anything else.' Not the sort of thing a man who has just ridden on a dirt gallop without goggles likes to hear, especially when 'Mr. Winter' is making a beeline for you in a determined manner. I preferred not to look but braced myself in anticipation of what was to follow. He trotted up with a wry grin, gave a friendly laugh and trotted on.

Mr. Winter and Oliver encouraged me to have another go and for the rest of my time at Cirencester I used to go over once or twice a week and ride out.

My second point-to point season was the 1979 one and I won the East Essex Hunt Race on Icy Affaire. Icy and myself were starting to get our act together, as we also managed a second in a hunter chase on 5th May at Folkestone. This was my first ride over proper National Hunt fences. The fences were noticeably bigger. It was particularly pleasing, despite being beaten thirty lengths by another East Anglian outfit, General Confusion, ridden by George Cooper. I managed to go past the horse ridden by Jim Wilson in the run-in to be second. Jim Wilson was already well-established as one of the leading amateurs in the country and was later to be one of the few amateurs to win the Gold Cup when he won on Little Owl in 1981.

My third point-to-point season, 1980, was the season I had left the Dennis's in Lincolnshire and gone home, when father had Icy Affaire and two other home-breds for me to ride. Icy ran his heart out and we managed to win two races in 1980, although the other two home-breds were, as they say, 'slow as boats' and did nothing but helped to establish my name as one of East Anglia's regular riders.

The next season, the 1981 point-to-point season, (which is part of the 1980/1981 National Hunt Season) was my last year at Cirencester, when I was having to work much harder, although I managed to clock up four wins from sixteen rides.

Two wins in February got things going well - Icy won on the 7th at Higham and Stoic Yarn on the 28th at Cottenham. Two incidents during the season gave me the breaks that one so badly needs to get a foot in the door. The first happened on a Bank Holiday weekend, well into the season. My half-brother, David and I always referred to Oliver as 'Yahweh' as we were constantly expected to live in awe of him. He had won the Sun Alliance Hurdle at the National Hunt Festival at Cheltenham on Venture To Cognac and, as far as we were concerned, the world worshipped him; it was always Oliver this, Oliver that, Oliver's fantastic and whenever I met people it was always 'you're Oliver's brother'. Oliver rang home on the Friday and told father that as he had nothing to ride under rules, he would come home for Marks Tey the next day and asked if some rides could be found for him. Imagine how I felt, I was working hard for my rides and Yahweh just rings up to get them.

In the maiden Oliver rode a horse called Straightlace; he was going extremely well ten lengths clear of the field and jumping like a buck, but

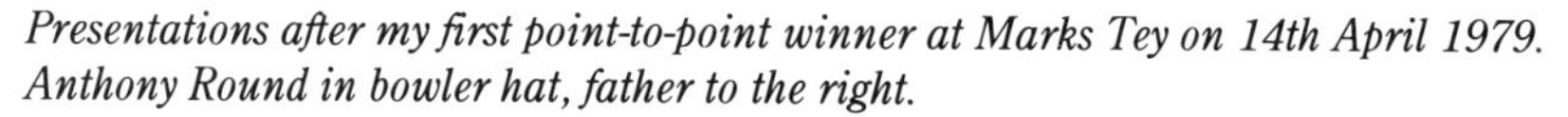

Presentations after my first point-to-point winner at Marks Tey on 14th April 1979. Anthony Round in bowler hat, father to the right.

Icy Affaire and I lead David Turner over the last to win our third point-to-point together - at Marks Tey on 5th April 1980.

Icy and I leading a big field on the way to victory on 7th February 1981 at Cottenham.

as he came to the last in the straight by the paddock, he tried to run out and went straight through the wing. No one seemed to be hurt and my initial thought was 'How terrible' but, remembering how angry I was with him, it changed to 'How funny, serves him right'.

Luckily everybody was alright. Oliver came up to me and said, 'You ought to get on that horse, he runs on Monday', to which I answered, 'F... off, I've just come back from a broken collar-bone.' But Oliver was adamant he would win, so I took the ride and he bolted up by ten lengths in a maiden at the Essex Farmers. We went down to Kent for the West Street Point-to-point in May, run at Aldington, near Ashford, and won again.

The second incident was when Libby Lees, one of the powerful forces in point-to-pointing, put me up on Florida King who was owned by Edna Hunnable. Florida King had been a prolific winner and amongst his victories was the Grand Marnier two years before.

Florida King was the most lovely horse but we didn't click first time and parted company. I can't exactly say how or why, but I broke my collarbone for the second time, which put me out for the rest of the season. Somehow I had done enough to impress Libby who, with a number of young horses to bring on, asked me to ride regularly for her the following season.

This was my last season with Icy, a true friend and a perfect first horse. Our record was four wins, three seconds and five thirds in point-to-points and a second in a hunter chase. He retired, became father's hack around the farm and everybody's pet, living until he was almost twenty-years old.

Newmarket and First Amateur Championship
September 1981 - June 1984

A fortuitous visit to a saddler's in Newmarket led to my first job after leaving Cirencester; assistant trainer to Harry Thomson Jones, better known as Tom Jones.

In my final year I was on the advanced farm management course. Unlike the 'gin and tonic' courses, this was a course for the dedicated farmer. There were only twenty of us on it and as it was continuous assessment, one had to concentrate and attend. Certainly the work was reasonably hard by anybody's standards.

One day, however, I needed a new saddle and while at Newmarket in Gibson's, I bumped into Di Haine, Tom Jones's daughter, who asked me what I was going to do when I finished my course. In all honesty I should have said, 'going back to Essex to farm', but I didn't. There looked to be more to this question than just polite conversation or passing the time of day, something might be in the offing, so instead I said, 'I don't know'.

I was right. Alex Stewart, Tom Jones's then assistant, was off to America for six months before starting up on his own and Di was wondering if I wanted to work for her father. It seemed a perfect opportunity. I had decided the next year was going to be my year, and the Point-to-point Championship would be going to me. I needed to be near Newmarket to ride Libby's horses, so what could be better than working there.

Within a month or so I was installed in Newmarket - living in Park Street with Teddy Beckett of the British Bloodstock Agency (B.B.A.) and working at Green Lodge. It was all a bit of a shock for the former Cirencester student who wasn't used to regular early starts and a full day's work. Luckily my experiences at Mr. Winter's and Libby's had at least steered me in the right direction, otherwise the whole thing might have proved too much for me.

It is an amazingly military set-up at Tom Jones's - everything is executed to precision timings, the turnout is immaculate and the stable routine, especially at evening stables, is second to none. There is no accepting second best. For instance, when you pull out, if the sheet is not square on the horse's back with the line straight down the middle, it is straight back in to sort it out. If a horse had been lying on its bed when you came to get it ready and had straw marks on the coat, they had to come out when you pulled out, otherwise it was straight back in to sort it out. Nothing was overlooked.

Tom Jones was not the easiest man I've worked for, but considering the number of silly mistakes I made, I'm astonished at how tolerant he was. In or around the yard he required a high standard of work and attention to detail.

One day I was holding two colts after we got back from exercise. One was Touching Wood, a leading contender for the Derby and subsequent winner of the St. Leger, the other was Princes Gate, who had just won a Group Three race. I didn't have a care in the world. I stood there, miles away, letting the two of them sniff one another. They must have been on the verge of striking out at one another when Tom Jones spotted me. Mad - the word isn't strong enough to describe the ensuing scene.

He was also a great leveller - any sign of cockiness and he would be on you. One day, I was holding his hack on the Heath when all of Stoute's and Cecil's strings trotted by. I felt frightfully smart, looking at all the girls who I could see were having a bit of a side-on glance to check who I was when, suddenly, out of the blue, came the most appalling bellow, 'For f...'s sake hold that horse properly!!'. It was the guv'nor, who was making very sure that not only did I know, but all of Newmarket knew, that he objected to the way I was holding his hack. I chose to ignore this outburst. I looked at the hack, the rein I was holding and my hand, and felt there was absolutely nothing wrong with what I was doing. In a less confident manner I continued to watch the passing strings. Seconds later came another ear-piercing scream along very much the same lines. I was now being subjected to great embarrassment in front of the two largest strings in Newmarket. Fortunately, without further ado, the head lad came to my rescue, telling me I should be holding both reins and not just one. That was the sort of detail Tom would pick up while doing something else and yes, there were moments when one loathed him, but he was a man whom I greatly admired and respected and I would never hear a bad word said against him outside the yard.

The head lad, Fred Flippance, who had been with Tom from the start, was a star. Standing well over six-foot tall and wiry in build, he was a tremendously hard worker who never seemed in a rush, never panicked and with whom I enjoyed many an hour's talk after work in the evening. Tragically he died of cancer in 1986.

Fred will be best remembered, not for being Tom Jones's head lad, but for his extraordinary association with his hack, the one time famous chaser, Tingle Creek. His popularity as a racehorse was earned by his slightly wild nature, which resulted in his desire to gallop his rivals into the ground from the moment the tapes went up, all of which was combined with an ability to jump like 'ten stags'. None of this madness was lost with age. If anything it got worse. His standing in the yard was unparalleled. It didn't matter if there were Classic winners in the yard, Tingle Creek came first; he was the most spoiled horse I have ever known. Any new idea was first tried out on Tingle, his box had every new gadget, every new accessory and Tingle was the best fed and best dressed horse in Newmarket. He loved all the attention and really played to it but, like all stars, he was a somewhat enigmatic character. Tingle overcame his idiosyncrasies by forming a bizarre relationship with Fred. They adored one another which was never more obvious than when the string would cross a road near the Heath. Fred and Tingle would stand in the middle of the road to stop the cars and the string would then cross. As the last horse crossed, Tingle would arch his neck round, look at Fred and wait to be given a polo mint, otherwise he would refuse to move.

Although I wasn't in Newmarket at the time, there was a famous occasion when Tingle got loose on the gallops. He behaved like a lunatic and galloped flat out, back down the Bury Road. Everybody recognised him and tried to stop him but he'd got himself into such a state he was beyond stopping. That was until Fred stood in the road, holding out a polo mint going 'Whoa!'. Tingle skidded along the tarmac to a halt.

My job was far less that of a pupil, than a fully fledged assistant. Arriving as I did in September, 1981, I only just caught the back-end of the flat season, and soon settled into the rather monotonous winter routine of an important flat stable. There was none of the glamour normally attached to being an assistant in my job; no racing, no work in the office and I certainly didn't have breakfast with the guv'nor. No, my job was a yard job. I started at 6.45 a.m. and would ride a racehorse first lot, changing to a hack for the second and third lots, finishing the morning at about midday. My real work would start at evening stables. Firstly, I was in charge of the hacks, all four of them - Tingle Creek, two very smart cobs and Park Ranger. I behaved like a lad. I set the beds 'fair' (a racing expression meaning a clean, tidy bed), 'dressed them over' (groomed) and hay, watered and fed them.

I found life in Newmarket fairly hectic - the early start, a liquid lunch in the Bedford Lodge, followed by evening stables and then, being a 'new boy' in Newmarket, the probability of dinner at someone's house. Why anyone ever bothered to invite me to dinner was quite beyond me, I would just about survive until 10.00 p.m. and then fall asleep.

It was a point of personal pride to master this problem; I needed an opportunity to get in a quick nap each day. Salvation came in the form of Park Ranger, one of the hacks. He was a marvellous old character, a bit light on teeth due to age so, no doubt to help the digestion, he would swing his head with a great rhythm between his hay and his water and back again, never having a mouthful without a drink. I soon perfected the art of getting the hacks out of the way quickly and being detached from the main yard, I would settle down in the corner of Park Ranger's box for the much needed nap. Such was the old horse's concern for my well-being that his routine changed, with an additional swing to the other side, after a drink to check I was alright. It was the change of routine that was responsible for me being caught by Fred. He couldn't understand why Parky was swinging to the other side and was so intrigued he had to have a look and there I was, curled up in the corner. Luckily Fred was a good mate and he totally understood my needs.

The sound of closing doors and Fred shouting at the staff to hurry up activated my mental alarm clock. It was approaching 5.30 p.m., time for Tom Jones to look round and my next job. Going around evening stables in most yards is a fairly drawn out affair but at Green Lodge it was more like changing the guard at Buckingham Palace. I led the entourage. My job was to go two boxes clear of the guv'nor, check the lad was ready and then put two drops of iodine in the water, something even I could manage without too many problems. Then he would follow, with Fred who carried the carrots - one for each inmate. Every box and every horse looked immaculate; sand and disinfectant had to be put down on the floor, a twist of straw in every doorway, tools laid out and every lad showed both sides of the horses he did. It was a rigorous inspection and woe betide anybody who was caught out. Finally the travelling head lad would bring up the rear, closing each door after the guv'nor. And so ended the day's work. As I left for Park Street my thoughts turned to the evening's activities and temporarily I became filled with zestful energy, something which had abandoned me since lunchtime and within a few hours was again to leave me.

I had to wait until my fifth point-to-point season, 1982, to make any real impression on the racing world. I was now to team up firmly with Libby Lees and in fact had more success hunter-chasing than I did point-to-pointing. Libby is an amazing person, formerly married to Nick Lees, Clerk of the Course at Newmarket, she is totally devoted to her horses and they come before anything else. She must be one of the best teachers for riders and horses available. Her record over the years, with either cheap or problem horses, speaks volumes for her ability as a trainer; she is thorough nearly to the point of obsession and her horses are invariably the best turned out at races. Like most perfectionists she expects the same of you and if she didn't feel you were pulling your weight, would lose no time in making it clear.

Tom Jones was an excellent employer for an aspiring amateur jockey and from the word go he allowed me to visit Libby's on a regular basis. Up until Christmas we were hunting or qualifying the horses and after Christmas I rode out regularly for her. The yard was only twelve miles away from Newmarket so Libby often brought the horses over there to work. With about fourteen horses in the yard the prospects for the forthcoming season looked good. I wasn't going to be allowed to ride the best horses from the yard, they remained with Lucy King, now Lucy Gibbons. However, luckily for me, a funny old character called Reliable Robert changed that. He was not the most genuine of individuals but I managed to win two point-to-points on him and from then on I rode the best horses as well.

My first success under Rules came the day after the National Hunt Festival at Cheltenham. I had gone down to see Oliver ride in the Gold Cup on father's horse, Venture To Cognac, trained by Fred Winter and I returned to East Anglia to ride at Fakenham on a lovely five-year-old horse, Lakin.

I remember the events leading up to the day nearly more than the day itself. A car load of us stopped off at the Swan Hotel in Moreton-in-the-Marsh for a sauna. They included Oliver, Paul Webber, now a director of the Curragh Bloodstock Agency (C.B.A.) and Nigel Twiston-Davies, who owned and trained that very good mare, Mrs. Muck. There was absolutely no need for me to have a sauna, but I pretended there was. I had never had one before. However, jockeys always needed them and if I was to ride a winner the next day I felt it was imperative I had one. So fortified, I drove to Fakenham fully prepared to ride my first winner under Rules - confidence was rising.

Lakin was a five-year-old who had had leg problems. He was a lovely big horse and was a class winner on the flat, but he had gone wrong and ended up at Libby's. He was a strong horse who took a hell of a hold, but luckily jumped like a stag although he would occasionally 'miss one out'. Prior to the Fakenham outing I had ridden him in point-to-points. The first time we had parted company, but the second time he had won really quite a nice race at Cottenham.

Winning my first race under Rules proper by twenty lengths; Lakin at Fakenham, 9th March 1982.

Being led in by Clare Villar on Mr. Mellors, one of my Cheltenham Double. Libby Lees in fur hat to the left, Nick Lees in brown hat to the right.

After the Cottenham win, a lot of the serious bloodstock agents like David Minton, then of the C.B.A., had offered his charming owner, Mrs. Clare Villar, substantial sums, so I was very glad that the Fakenham race turned out something of a formality. We won by twenty lengths hard held.

The scorecard for the season was, even though I say so myself, very impressive. Four wins from thirty-four point-to-point rides but, far more importantly, I had nine wins from seventeen rides under Rules proper, including the never to be forgotten double at the Cheltenham Hunters Meeting in May on Mr. Mellors and Lakin both trained by Libby Lees and owned by Clare Villar. These were my first two rides at Cheltenham and, like Fakenham, it was to turn out to be one of my lucky courses and, not unnaturally therefore, one of my favourites.

During my first year with Tom Jones I had hoped to win the Point-to-point Championship. I didn't, but my nine wins under Rules were very

Lakin could leave the odd one out. We stayed united to win the Baxter's Landrover Hunter Chase at Fakenham on the 12th April 1982, giving Libby Lees her 100th winner.

encouraging and the next season, rather grandly, I set my sights on winning the Amateur Riders Championship which had fallen to Oliver in the 1979/1980 season.

Oliver was a great help; he was certainly responsible for getting me some of the rides which eventually brought about the turn in my riding career - from an unheard of amateur to reasonably successful amateur in the season 1982/1983. My nine successes the previous season were all on hunter-chasers against other amateurs. I now needed to get rides from professional trainers in races open to professionals.

Probably the first ride Oliver got for me was the most significant, Springfield Cracker at Newton Abbott on 31st August 1982 in the Taw Amateur Riders Handicap Hurdle for John Jenkins. Oliver couldn't do the weight, so he asked me if I wanted to ride. By luck more than good judgement I finished third, beaten three-quarters of a length and a neck, and a delighted John Jenkins asked me if I would ride for him again. I ended the season riding three winners for him, including two on Springfield Cracker, both at Plumpton. He was to become one of the most important trainers of my riding career.

In November Oliver dislocated his shoulder and kindly presented me with two important rides from Fred Winter's stable. I should say that Mr. Winter always has been 'Sir' or 'Guv'nor' to me and is one of the greatest individuals ever to grace the National Hunt scene. As a struggling amateur, it was a big step forward to be riding for one of the most powerful stables ever.

In mid-November I rode a horse called Roller Coaster at Ascot for the Winter stable and was beaten by a head in a photo finish by Ballyross ridden by Tim Thomson Jones (son of my employer). I probably should have won, but I let Roller Coaster down, flopping about a bit up the run-in. Mr. Winter kindly patted me on the shoulder as I unsaddled and said 'well done'. I can't think that he meant it.

A week later Oliver's injury presented me with, at that stage, my most exciting riding offer - Venture To Cognac at Newbury in the Jacky Upton Chase. It was an offer I couldn't refuse; it was my chance to shine on a top-class track in front of a very knowledgeable crowd. I had no need to shine (assuming I was capable of shining). I sat there, letting Venture do it all and we bolted up, ironically beating John Francome on Silversmith, who would have had the ride, if father hadn't kindly given me the ride on his horse.

At Christmas, I still hoped to win the amateur title, based on the belief that Libby's powerful string of hunters, with the likes of Lakin, Corked, Mr. Mellors and Reliable Robert, would carry me through to the title with a spate of wins in the last months of the season. Sadly it was not to be - I hadn't set the racing world alight and seriously thought of giving it all up. By the end of the season I had ridden thirteen winners from seventy-two rides, finished fourth in the table of amateur riders. I also clocked up five winners in point-to-points. I was rather disillusioned with the whole thing. I left Tom Jones and went back to Essex to consider the future.

Before going to Ireland to work for Arthur Moore, Oliver had done a spell with Gavin Pritchard-Gordon in Newmarket. Oliver encouraged me to have one more crack and, as father had been associated with the yard for a number of years as an owner, Gavin kindly agreed that I could go and work as a pupil assistant. Although regarded as a flat trainer, he also has a small but successful string of jumpers, which I hoped would act as a launching pad in my final quest for the title.

After the disappointments of the previous season, the 1983/1984 season was going to be my last serious challenge for the amateur title and, if I failed, I had already accepted mentally that I would return to Essex to farm, in the knowledge that I had given race-riding my best shot.

Gavin Pritchard-Gordon, Old Radleian, served his apprenticeship with Harvey Leader at Shalfleet in Newmarket. He had instant success when he took on the yard, with the likes of Ardoon, Record Run and Trillium, but he then moved a little way up the Bury Road, into Lord Derby's former yard, Stanley House, without doubt one of Newmarket's most attractive set-ups.

It was a joy to work for Gavin. He is certainly one of the most popular trainers in racing, always prepared to have a laugh at anything, not least himself. I think the year I spent with Gavin was not only my most enjoyable in racing, but also one in which I learned a great deal about the game in general. The name 'pupil assistant' covers a multitude of sins. There is no definitive description, suffice to say you are normally something of a dogsbody, pandering to the needs of either the head lad, or the fully fledged assistant. Fortunately this was not the case at Stanley House. I was treated with a certain amount of respect and my responsibilities went considerably further than looking after the hacks and putting iodine into the water. Luckily I only weighed around 9st. 7lbs. 'in my socks' as they say, so in the morning I joined the hallowed ranks of the 'work rider', while the afternoon was taken up in the totally new world of the 'office'. As a pupil assistant you begin to feel very grown up when you are allowed into the office - for it is in this room, filled with modern technology, you learn about such important aspects of racing as entries and the handicapping of horses.

There is one strong school of thought within the racing industry which considers that a very sound knowledge of both entering, and then deciding whether or not to run, is the key to success; the argument being that it doesn't matter how fit an individual is, if it is running in the wrong company it will not win. Since my days with Gavin, the entering system has changed. In my day it was the old three-week system but now it has changed to the 'five day system'.

Regardless of the system, there is a certain skill in entering horses, and saving owners money with unnecessary entries in races which have a habit of producing a 'good one', or will simply be too competitive. All this can only be learned with practice and at Stanley House I was getting a good grounding in the subject. Likewise the handicapping. This involved thumbing through a number of publications, not least the formbook, and coming up with an objective conclusion. Was the individual horse 'well in' or not? The military expression 'time spent in reconnaissance is never wasted', could not be better attributed to this very problem. Some good homework could make all the difference between success and failure.

It was, however, in my new found role as a work rider that I began to grasp a facet of race-riding hitherto lost on me - pace. There is no better way of learning about the pace of horses than to ride work with good flat jockeys who have a built-in speedometer. I was extremely fortunate to have George Duffield as a work partner, an experience that definitely stood me in good stead later.

Judgement of pace is essential in a jockey's make-up. In recent years, two jockeys have been brilliant examples - Steve Cauthen on the flat and Peter Scudamore over jumps. Both have won an extraordinary number of races from the front, judging the pace to perfection; it is a skill that can be exploited to great effect for the ability to go at an even pace is, on the whole, far more preferable to suddenly asking your horse for a surge of speed, an energy sapping exercise that has to be detrimental to the individual's capabilities.

My early ventures up the many and varied gallops at Newmarket were obviously deemed satisfactory, for Gavin took the unprecedented

Gavin Pritchard-Gordon.

step of asking me to ride on the flat. He gave me some great rides, the first of which was Jorge Miguel (who subsequently won the Bic Hurdle at Lingfield) at Newmarket, finishing second. I then followed up with two winners, Pass to Paradise and the second on a horse called Khyber at Brighton. While it was a great thrill to ride a winner, the day will always stick in my mind as another 'first'. It is rather like being awarded your colours at school; you know you have got there when, as a pupil, you are asked to 'saddle up' at the races. This job gives you a new sphere of responsibility. A badly put on saddle could easily alter the entire course of events during the race; a saddle slipping back could not only endanger the jockey, it virtually guarantees that any chance of victory is ruined. On top of which, if the horse does win, you are then confronted by the press.

On another day at Brighton, the latter problem proved my downfall. The horse in question, Wiveton, owned by Lord Derby, bolted up and the press were keen to know all. My enthusiasm to impress got the better of me and I started to tell them about another of Lord Derby's horses which would run well the next day. I succeeded in my quest to impress for there, on the front page of *The Sporting Life* the next day, was a quote from 'S.Sherwood, Gavin Pritchard-Gordon's assistant'. The only problem - a fairly major one - was that the horse was in fact owned by one of Gavin's principal American owners and not by Lord Derby!

Life outside racing in Newmarket was pretty fast, with the likes of Willie Jarvis and William Haggas (he doesn't like to be called Willie) to name only two, as fellow assistant trainers. Luckily I shared a house with an old friend, James Lambert, at Fordham, just outside Newmarket, so when I wanted to keep a lower profile and go to ground, I could do so without being pestered. There was no shortage of jokers and you had to be continually on your guard. If you weren't so before, you soon became fairly 'streetwise'. On one occasion I got home, having been to dinner with a girlfriend at Gavin's, only for the 'phone to ring. It was Ian Robertson, of rugby fame, being mischievous. Jane (the girlfriend) and I decided revenge had to be sought there and then, so off we went to his house and managed, by good luck rather than good judgement, to attract the attention of the Pritchard-Gordon's childrens' very pretty nanny, Juliette.

The plot was set, she would inveigle Robertson to the back door on some spurious pretence where, hiding in the bushes, were Jane and myself armed with one bucket of water and some flour. Everything went according to plan, water and flour hitting the target. The one oversight on my part was the 'get-away'. I had forgotten Ian was a Scottish three-quarter, but it only took me thirty yards to remember.

Don't let anybody tell you that Newmarket isn't a thirsty place - a large amount of furious drinking takes place. Very little excuse is needed, but I tried to avoid drinking if I was riding the next day. It didn't always work. The day before I rode Reliable Robert in the Foxhunters at Liverpool, I ran into Willie Jarvis, who was then Henry Cecil's assistant, and he suggested 'a quick one' in the pub. I stupidly agreed. In the pub we met one of Cecil's lads, Yarmy, (one of the best boxers in the history of lads' boxing) and that was it. Three hours later Willie and myself tried to ride down the High Street, in tandem, on a bicycle. I was in charge of the steering, Willie the pedalling; there was little to compare with the Tour de France for style and technique as one bend proved too much. We hit the kerb and shot straight through a shop window. Thirty seconds later Willie grunted something about being alright. On the other hand I cracked a finger (no pun intended!). All I could think about was my ride at Liverpool the next day and all Willie could think about was his intended ride, had we reached our proposed destination.

Although not the most genuine of horses, Reliable Robert gave me a great ride around the Aintree Grand National Course. We led for most of the way and he only weakened three fences out. A good first ride at a course, especially at Aintree, always puts you in the right frame of mind for later visits.

The Stable Lads' Boxing at the Grosvenor House Hotel in London

My first time over Becher's - a lovely jump from Reliable Robert as we lead the field in the 1984 Foxhunters.

proved to be another of my less successful social outings. The evening is a big social event in the racing world, (dinner, speeches, etc. before the boxing) and has been the subject of adverse media coverage, mainly due to a very biased film crew who went all out to portray a yuppie image of, 'let's get pissed and sod everyone else'. What they failed to do was remind viewers that the whole evening is designed to raise money for the stable lads' cause.

I was on a very wild table with everyone out to make the most of the evening. After the boxing we went clubbing and came across a few of what might best be described as 'dubious girls', who seemed more than happy to go back to one of the party's flat. Paul Webber and I formed the advance party but couldn't get into the flat, so were forced to wait on the landing. There it was, crying out to be taken off the wall, pleading in fact to be used - yes, the fire extinguisher. Twenty minutes later the rest of the party arrived and, having got into position, I waited for the first unfortunate to come up the stairs and round the corner. Tragically, it was a black woman wearing a mink coat. That proved to be no deterrent and soon she was covered in water. But worse still she was wearing a wig which gave up the unequal struggle against the jet of water and flew off and down the stairs.

She turned and followed her wig, shouting and screaming, with me in hot pursuit trying to apologize. She would not listen to reason (what ever reason there was) and instead shouted hysterically at me and, to press her point, hit me over the head with her shoe. As luck would have it, a couple of policemen outside saw what was happening, but they did little to calm the woman. It came as some surprise when a solicitor's letter arrived four days later claiming £4,000 for damage to the coat. I had never come across anything like this before, so turned to my father for advice. He thought the whole thing was terribly funny, asked his solicitor to write a strong letter back and that was the end of the whole episode.

The 1983/1984 season started well for me thanks to the assistance of John Jenkins, Toby Balding and Philip Mitchell. My first winner came for Philip on 12th August when Zaccio won at Plumpton. He held on by a short diminishing half length from Admiral Grenville, ridden by John Francome, who had been champion jockey for four of the last five seasons. John was always hard to beat in a tight finish and it was a great start to the season.

Toby Balding then gave me a good break on a little chestnut, French

Zaccio at Plumpton - my first winner in the 1983/1984 season. We just held on to beat John Francome by a diminishing half-length.

Rodney Parade gave me three important wins when chasing the Amateur Riders Championship in April/May 1984, seen at Hexham.

bred horse called Sanhedrin and I was to win five out of six times on him in a few weeks. The first win came on 9th September at Newton Abbot where we won the valuable 'Horse and Hound West Country Challenge Cup', an amateur riders' hurdle race, carrying 9 st. 13 lbs.. It is always a hotly contested race with a good number of runners. For some reason *Raceform*, in their annual formbook, decided to refer to me as Miss S. Sherwood, which I think is a bit unfair. Our fifth win came on the 19th December at Ascot where once again we won another amateur riders hurdle, this time carrying 11 st. .

Sanhedrin was an exciting horse to ride over two-and-a-half to two-and-three-quarters miles, as he had to be held up and used to come with a great burst over the last two or three furlongs. The correct distance was absolutely critical - two miles was too short and he didn't quite get the three miles.

Unfortunately, one Dermot Browne was associated with Michael Dickinson's very powerful yard in the north and had stolen the march, going eight clear in December. That, for an amateur, is a figure virtually impossible to bridge, but John Jenkins kept my end up, continuing to supply me with winners.

Once the hunter chase season starts in February, the number of amateur races increases, especially during April and May when there are a few amateur only meetings. Misfortune struck Dermot Browne when he had a bad fall on 23rd April, Easter Monday, from Sausolito at Market Rasen and broke his left arm. I must confess I was delighted when I heard the news - I only had to ride twenty-six winners to win the title and the prospect of Dermot riding again that season seemed very slim.

Rodney Parade will always hold a very special place in my heart. He could not have been a more genuine horse. He was sent by John Jenkins all over the country to help me in my quest for the title. On Saturday, 28th April, we won an amateur riders handicap hurdle at Hexham; the following Thursday, 3rd May, we went in by fifteen lengths over three miles at Hereford and eight days later, on Friday, 11th May, we were back up north at Sedgefield, winning again.

A double at Folkestone on 15th May and another winner at Stratford on 19th May all helped and my next real opportunity to close the gap came with the amateur meeting at Fakenham on 28th May. It was imperative I got the best rides available and, having fixed myself up, I passed any other rides I was offered onto Oliver. It ended up being quite a day for the

Toby Balding.

Sherwoods. I rode the last three winners and Oliver chased me home once. Suspicious as it might seem, I can assure you there was our normal quota of brotherly rivalry. It is not often anyone, let alone an amateur, wins three consecutive races and, just for the record, my hat-trick was firstly the Toby Balding trained Faithful Don, followed by Midsummer Special from Dave Thom's Newmarket yard and Mrs. Villar's Corked.

The lead was being whittled down. I only needed three winners to clinch the championship and two to tie and I had two fancied rides at Uttoxeter the next day - Rockfield Boy and Easterly Gael for John Jenkins. Uttoxeter has never been a particular favourite of mine and that day it reached a new low in my prejudiced view. Rockfield Boy looked like a winner but tripped at the third last flight giving me concussion and a three-day statutory holiday. I walked around the course for thirty minutes before I started to remember anything. That is why I am a great believer in not cutting corners with your head. If you have concussion, count yourself lucky and take the holiday. It annoyed me whenever I heard someone in the weighing room trying to avoid the doctor, as it has always struck me as being so short-sighted.

Easterly Gael won, ridden by Jonjo O'Neill who, characteristically, rang me that evening at home to find out if I was alright and to say that if he could help me with a winning ride before the end of the season, in my chase for the championship, he would do so. Three days' holiday when you need three winners seems a lifetime. Luckily Gavin let me ride Dhofar at Stratford on the Friday night, the day before the end of the season, and he won comfortably. There was one day left, two meetings and I needed two winners. I had to do it. Dermot had already won the title twice and word had it that he was resting on his laurels, assuming he had won it again.

Rarely have I been so determined and with the help of both Coral Pritchard-Gordon and David Nicholson, the final day's rides were fixed.

The day went as follows:

3.35 p.m. Stratford. Rode Star Charter for John Jenkins who finished fifth.

4.00-5.45 p.m. Accompanied by Oliver we leave Stratford heading for Market Rasen. A record-breaking drive up the A46, a journey that usually takes well over two hours.

6.30 p.m. Jonjo O'Neill, one of the game's true gentlemen, gives up the ride on Vitingo in the Abbey Selling Hurdle and I win by ten lengths.

7.05 p.m. A slight setback; Coral Pritchard-Gordon knew the owners of Manston Marauder, trained by Jimmy Fox. She rang the owners in Oman for the ride but the implacable Jimmy Fox stood by his claimer, Stan Moore, who duly won.

8.20 p.m. Gordon Chambers returned from walking the course and confirmed I would ride his Richard G in the final race of the season, the Final Fling Novices Chase. Jimmy Frost was down to ride but very kindly and generously gave up the ride for me, demonstrating the camaraderie among the N.H. jockeys.

9.05 p.m. Richard G bolted up. The only danger in the race was

The last race of the season - Richard G winning to give me my first Amateurs Championship.

another amateur, Norman Babbage, and although in the final analysis I won on the bridle, I was so nervous at the third and second last fences that I thought I was going to be beaten, just through sheer anxiety. No small race has ever meant more to anyone than that did to me.

The return journey took longer than normal and after a few stops we eventually got back to Oliver's house in Lambourn at 3.00 a.m.. In the meantime Dermot had been celebrating all night, completely unaware of the final result!

The last flight in the Horse & Hound Cup 1983 winning on Sanhedrin.

The last flight in the Horse & Hound Cup 1984. I fall on Star Charter.

Lambourn and Second Amateur Championship
July 1984 - June 1985

Subconsciously I felt my ambitions in racing had reached a climax. I had gone into it to have some fun, set myself a target to be amateur champion, which I had achieved, and by rights I should have now returned to Essex to take control of the farm. I had four years of Cirencester and three years at Newmarket behind me, and I'm sure my father was hoping the racing bug would now leave me and that I would come to terms with the prospect of being a farmer.

While I had every intention of going home to farm, I cannot deny I enjoyed the life of an amateur jockey; I had built up a mass of friends, travelled here, there and everywhere, and had a lot of fun. The prospect of going back to Essex to farm seemed a trifle dull in comparison, further to which I was offered the most enormous 'carrot' by Oliver.

Oliver was about to set out on his training career. He had bought Rhonehurst, a lovely racing stable in Upper Lambourn, formerly owned by Captain Richard Head who sent out such good horses as Border Incident and Uncle Bing from there. The house was superb, with thirty boxes and two cottages, all set in sixty acres.

The previous season had been my last point-to-pointing and Terry Selby of *Point-to-Pointers and Hunter Chasers* tells me my record was eighteen wins, thirteen seconds and twelve thirds. *Point-to-Pointers and Hunter Chasers* was, at one time, one of my favourite books as they were one of the first to sing my praises as a rider. I parted from Libby Lees, who has now re-married and is called Libby Heath. She has moved to Royston and taken out a full licence. I had hoped to ride for her again in my last season, but it never worked out.

A great first ride in the Grand National. Corbiere leads me and Musso at Becher's.

17

The time was right for Oliver to start. He had spent five years with Fred Winter, had won the Amateur Riders Championship and had ridden such good horses as Venture To Cognac, Rolls Rambler and Donegal Prince, to name but a few. He was now a married man, having taken the sensible step the year before of marrying his employer's daughter, Denise, better known as Sneeze, and with Rhonehurst on the market it seemed a superb opportunity to branch out on his own. Sneeze having been a high-powered event rider and having been born and bred into racing, was more than qualified to be a trainer's wife.

Oliver could not have hoped for more - he started with a first-class yard and a good staff which included Chris Clarke, as professional a head lad as you could find. With the perfect trainer's wife there seemed little room for anyone else, but Oliver asked me to come and help, as assistant and amateur jockey. The lure was too great; I would be sad to leave Newmarket but, if I was going to stay in racing, there could be nothing better for the conscience than working for one's brother. Also, if I was going to have another go at the amateur title then Lambourn seemed an ideal place to be based. I accepted, no doubt much to father's displeasure, and was fully aware that when it came to the rides John Francome was number one.

Leaving Newmarket was sad, especially leaving Stanley House and Gavin and Coral Pritchard-Gordon, who between them had made life so much fun, carrying on right to the end by very kindly giving me a farewell party for about fifty people. Just before I left Newmarket I at least had a new mate. A rather short-legged, hairy, black and brown coloured companion, who was very long suffering and soon became familiar with every racecourse in England as he was my constant travelling companion. His name is Herbert and he is a black and tan terrier. He was given to me by Oliver and Sneeze, having been bred by Sneeze's grandmother, Mrs. Norah Pearson. She had brought the line back from Ireland with her, as it had originated in the 'Black and Tan Kennels'.

Fontwell was Herbert's favourite track, as there was a field next to the car park with an abundance of rabbits, while the likes of Kempton were very ordinary, Herbie being restricted to sniffing around the tarmac.

I was always slightly worried when I took Herbie racing with me that I might be carted off to hospital and Herbert left locked in my car. He was so well known in the weighing room however, I was fairly certain someone would have got him out, although it may not have done the car windows any good.

Life in Lambourn was very different, almost totally due to Baytree Cottage, the house I lived in about two miles outside Lambourn in East Garston. It was owned by Mark Bradstock, at that time assistant to Fulke Walwyn but now a trainer in his own right, and sharing the house was Sara Lawrence, the daughter of Lord Oaksey, the Channel 4 presenter. I had met Mark before, small in stature, always smiling and a great optimist, but Sara was something altogether new.

I must say I had been warned; I'd been told that Mark, when he arrived in Lambourn having done a short spell at the Guards Depot, Pirbright, was renowned for his tidiness and smart appearance but within two weeks Sara, his girlfriend, had reduced him and the cottage to a shambles. The cottage looked wonderful from the outside, but such was the disorganisation inside, it was discussed nationally! I was prepared for anything, or so I thought. Walking up the stairs for the first time I came face to face with a naked body, the one belonging to Sara Lawrence. I, as you might expect, was covered in embarrassment. Not Sara, she introduced herself, welcomed me and strutted past me en route to the bathroom and the scales. She then complained, not understanding why her weight hadn't gone down. While complaining she turned round and, from a distance, it was very clear why her weight hadn't gone down but I felt having just met her, albeit with no clothes on, it would be rude to tell her.

We all got on extremely well and in fact Mark was to become one of my closest friends. We all had a great deal in common; a similar outlook on life, fiercely competitive natures, a love of racing and we all enjoyed a relaxed evening at home.

The march of time is amazing. On my first morning at Rhonehurst, Oliver's yard, there were all of ten horses, mucked out by the staff including Oliver and Sneeze. To think it has now grown into a yard capable of housing seventy plus horses. The place was vibrant with excitement and it presented a challenge to me; it was no longer a case of thinking solely in terms of myself, I was there to help Oliver. Everything was new to me: the village, the yard, the gallops, in fact the only thing that wasn't new to me was the horse I rode out. Zaccio, who had been such a good work horse for me the previous season when trained by Philip Mitchell, was sent to Rhonehurst by the owners in an attempt to give Oliver a good start.

Zaccio was Oliver's first runner but his training career got off to an inauspicious beginning. Over-zealousness on my part trying to get Oliver off the mark proved fatal. We were at Newton Abbot, one of the tightest courses in the country. It was a big field and Zaccio made a terrible mistake, leaving me far too much to do. Instead of biding my time, I tried to go up the inside. I was never going to get through although I can count myself lucky in some respects - I found myself upsides Steve Smith-Eccles, who had every right to drill me into the railings, but fortunately, as a friend, he let me in.

My luck soon ran out; riding Star Charter in the Horse and Hound Cup at Newton Abbot I fell and broke a cheek-bone. It necessitated going to hospital, in this case R.A.F. Wroughton, near Swindon. Having a broken cheek-bone I couldn't drive (you would be amazed what an important part the cheek plays when driving!) so was very kindly driven there by Paul Croucher, one of the nicest, most amusing, not to mention able, jockeys in the weighing room who tragically died in a car accident in 1988.

At the hospital I was given the encouraging news that I had to lie on my back for two days. However, the ordeal was greatly enhanced by the appearance of an extremely attractive nurse. In no time at all I was madly in love; 'behind every cloud is a silver lining', as they say and had I not broken my cheek-bone I would never have met this gorgeous creature.

Me with my broken cheek-bone.

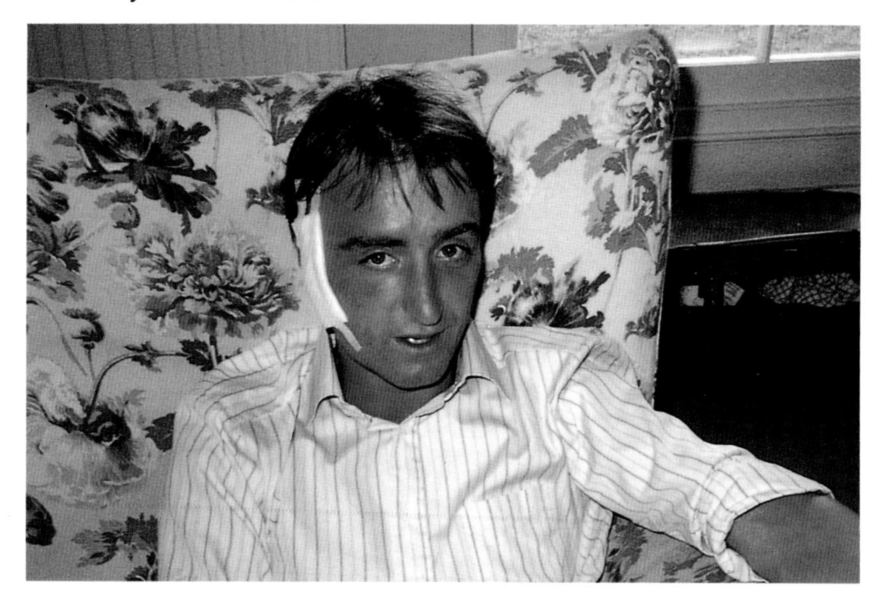

An important win for the Brothers Sherwood. The Breener at Newbury in November 1984.

Every time she came to treat me I was tempted to tell her. I even plotted an evening out for dinner, deciding that the best time to approach her with the invitation was on my last day, and then it happened. No, her husband didn't walk in, neither did her boyfriend. No, far worse - she told me I needed a suppository. That was embarrassing enough but when I realized she was going to administer it herself (to use a medical expression), all my self respect had gone. I couldn't look her in the eye and my two-day love affair had come to a sad end.

Oliver has a wonderful attitude towards racing, but by the middle of November things were just beginning to get to him. We were all trying hard, the early season horses were running well and getting placed but the all important winner eluded the Sherwood brothers. I had managed to ride a few winners for other stables, so was under slightly less pressure.

14th November 1984 was to be one of the more important landmarks for both Oliver and myself. The Breener, owned by R.E.A. Bott (Wigmore Street) Ltd., finally got Oliver off the mark at, very appropriately, Newbury. The owner of the company, David Bott, had horses with Fred Winter and was extremely generous in his support for Oliver. He showed supreme confidence in Oliver from the outset and spent a lot of money buying The Breener from Arthur Moore in Ireland. It is therefore not difficult to understand the pleasure The Breener's victory gave Oliver - not only was it his first, it was also for a very special owner. (It was a great shock to us all when David Bott died, whilst I was correcting the proofs of this book; he will be missed in many circles.)

The significance of the race was, for me, like Oliver, twofold. The fact I was allowed the horse in the first place meant a great deal to me. Oliver had hoped to secure the services of John Francome, but Fred Winter had a runner in the same race so Oliver had to look elsewhere. I didn't have the courage to ask. It was Mr. Bott's only horse in the yard and I felt it was unfair on Oliver to put myself forward. In the past I had ridden a horse called Musso for Mr. Bott but it still came as a great surprise when he asked me to ride The Breener. He was considered the best horse in the yard probably more on account of his value than his homework. His regular work rider was the travelling head lad, Cameron, who had 'done' Brown Chamberlin when he worked for Fred Winter. He therefore knew the feel of a good horse, but he is the type of man who is quiet and rarely, if ever, gets over-excited about anything. Whatever The Breener had done at home had been kept very close to his chest because he duly skated up at Newbury. Instead of riding a proven horse to victory, I had, for the first time, ridden a potentially brilliant horse.

He went on to win his next two races at Newbury in fine fashion and ended up third in the Supreme Novices' Hurdle at the Festival. In retrospect, he probably should have been run in the two-and-a-half mile hurdle, the Sun Alliance. He was a lovely horse, with plenty of class and he actually deserved to win at Cheltenham.

Once The Breener had set the standard, Oliver's season went from strength to strength with horses such as Taqdir, Arctic Warbler and Pukka Major all winning their races on the better courses. But the highlight of the season came at Cheltenham, in March, in the Kim Muir. David Nicholson offered me the ride on Charter Party, a subsequent Gold Cup winner, owned by Raymond and Jenny Mould, close friends of mine. I have to admit I semi-accepted the ride, then Fred Winter rang and asked me to ride Glyde Court, owned by Chris Cronin. It was one of those impossible situations; had it been any other trainer I would have turned the ride down but to be offered a ride by Fred Winter is something very special and the wish of every jockey, no disrespect to David Nicholson. I accepted the ride on Glyde Court and turned down Charter Party.

Baytree Cottage was represented in force. All three of us rode in the race and, so that no one felt lonely, we all came to the first in a little group, up with the leaders. Why Mark ever married Sara I will never understand - as we jumped the first Mark, through no fault of his own, bumped Sara. The tirade of abuse that followed is unrepeatable! Glyde Court managed to avoid Mark's slightly errant riding and seemed undeterred by Sara's language. He was a 'perfect' ride; well-mannered, a strong galloper and a lovely jumper who stayed forever, all the perfect ingredients to win the tough three-mile chase. The feeling as I went past the winning post in front was one of total euphoria - I had won a race at the National Hunt Festival.

That success had a big impact on me, slightly altering my perspective on race-riding. I was in with a chance of winning my second amateur title and my success on Glyde Court had the same effect as engaging the turbo on a car.

Vanity is something jockeys are constantly being accused of, really on account of watching themselves on video tapes. If that is the case, then I was certainly very vain after the Kim Muir. The tape with the race on it eventually wore out! But, having said that, video tapes are a great asset to jockeys - you learn an enormous amount watching yourself and they are, without doubt, the best medium for improving style. However, they are the cause of many embarrassing moments - dedication to the job is frequently confused with vanity when a close friend catches you watching the same race for the third time in a day.

By Cheltenham time I had just crept clear of Peter Dun in the amateur table, but sadly Peter had a bad fall in the New Year and was forced to retire, leaving the championship fairly open. Tim Thomson Jones, an 'also ran', as I like to remind him, until the serious amateurs gave up, was only seven winners behind me but, with the likes of Oliver, Fred Winter and John Jenkins, winners were steadily coming in.

I had my first ride in the Grand National on another horse from Mr. Winter's stable, Musso. I had a tremendous ride round in the front, or near the front, for the first circuit or so, but we ran out of puff and pulled up before the nineteenth.

One trainer who provided me with a winner was none other than Gay Kindersley, who has now sadly given up training. There can be few people in the world, let alone racing, who are as popular as Gay; he is the epitome of a gentleman, a wonderfully kind man without an enemy in the world. With such attributes you would think luck would run with the person - not with Gay, some drama always seems to befall him.

I rode Rix Woodcock for him at my luckiest, not to mention most successful racecourse, Fakenham, in a selling hurdle. I duly won but, to the horror of Gay and the owners, by ten lengths. Owners can never understand sellers and in this case the syndicate owners were completely lost on the intricacies of buying a horse back. Due to my over-enthusiastic victory Gay had to pay twice the odds. Fifty per cent of the owners couldn't understand why they had been sent a bill for winning a race and pulled out. A typically Gay situation! (See editor's note, page 157)

I quietly eased into Lambourn life and soon felt very much at home. There might be many differences between Newmarket and Lambourn, but entertainment is certainly not one of them. I managed to keep out of any trouble until a dinner party at the beginning of February at Rhonehurst. It was to celebrate Sneeze's and Jim Wilson's birthday. Jim,

Glyde Court winning the Kim Muir at the 1985 Cheltenham National Hunt Festival; my first Festival Winner.

Jenny Pitman's front gate with one of the famous cockerels.

who trains near Cheltenham, is a great friend, not only of Oliver's but a number of the Lambourn locals, and quite a crowd sat down for dinner, including Nicky Henderson, the Francomes, Tim Thomson Jones and Jimmy Duggan.

It all got out of control very quickly and for post-dinner entertainment it was decided to steal Jenny Pitman's two large cockerels which stand proudly cemented to the gate-posts at the entrance to her yard. All very silly and childish but, at the time, thought to be terribly funny. Tim Thomson Jones, Jimmy Duggan and I were despatched on a mission to retrieve at least one of the cockerels and then, when we got back, to forcibly hold Henderson, who was at the time *persona non grata* with Jenny, against the poor ornament and take a photograph to use for blackmail purposes.

Jenny's cockerels are large and very heavy. Considering some of the guests at dinner, the three chosen men were probably not the right ones for the job. We each took it in turns to try and move one of the wretched birds, giggling nervously like little schoolgirls and thinking that at any moment Jenny would appear. Fortunately she didn't and after what seemed an eternity we struggled back to the car with our trophy. Henderson realized what the plan was and fought for his life. We were now left with one homeless cockerel. Out of a host of potential homes, the grit bin half-way between Oliver's and Jenny's won the vote and there the cockerel stayed for the night, ready to inspect everybody riding past the next morning.

That was the end of it as far as we were concerned. Not for Jenny. History has shown her to be a pretty determined lady and this was going to be no exception; Burrough Hill Lad's preparation for another crack at the Gold Cup could almost have been waived in favour of finding the culprits. Two days later word in the village had it that Thomson Jones, Sherwood and Duggan had 'done it', only to be followed by Jenny confronting Oliver on the gallops and demanding that the culprits owned up, otherwise there would be trouble, i.e. the heavies would move in. The three of us had expended so much energy moving the cockerel we really weren't up to meeting the heavies, so we owned up.

We were ushered into a room and there, sitting behind a large desk, was Jenny, looking at her most menacing. Immediately, memories of D.R.W. Silk at Radley came flooding back. To add to the excitement, I took a mini tape-recorder in with me, a decision which nearly brought about my total downfall.

'I expected that of you,' she scowled, looking at Tim, then looking at me, she continued, 'I'm disappointed with you'. After looking at Jimmy for a moment she said, 'and who the hell are you?', which might have been the most painful punishment of all as he'd recently arrived as the new boy at Winter's, having enjoyed tremendous success, especially in the north.

Understandably, I think Jenny would be best described as 'upset' during our talking to. Had she heard the tape-recorder rewinding furiously as a result of me pushing the wrong button, she would no doubt have been even more upset. Luckily she didn't, solely on account of Tim quickly grasping the situation by the horns and answering her back very loudly. She ended up imposing her own fine on all of us, £125 each, to be paid to the Injured Jockeys Fund. Jenny is now a good friend, I hope.

One of the advantages of being an amateur is the opportunities it presents for riding abroad, especially if you are involved with F.E.G.E.N.T.R.I., the European Amateur Championship. In my capacity as Secretary of the

Amateur Riders Association I had to go over to Stockholm, with Tim Thomson Jones, Gay Kindersley and John Hislop for the Annual General Meeting.

We were looked after in regal fashion, with hardly a dull moment. All this weighed heavily against us on our final day, Sunday, when Tim and I were to ride at Taby. To set us right we opted for pre-lunch cocktails and after 3.00 p.m. I had no idea if it was New York or New Year. Gay, an inveterate punter, had worked out I was on a likely winner which needed backing.

We arrived at Taby and I was promptly sent off to walk the straw course, in a temperature of -6 degrees centigrade wearing only a shirt, in an attempt to sober me up. The plan worked - I sobered up and we 'shovelled' it on the Tote. We overdid it. In the paddock the owners were so mystified by the appalling price that they asked me to give the horse a 'sympathetic' ride. We won by three lengths, much to the delight of the English contingent, but not to the owners'. We had to carry Gay to the aeroplane, where he slept solidly for two hours!!

I also went abroad twice when an amateur to ride in the German 'Grand National' which was confined to amateurs. Each time I was second to Tim Thomson Jones. The first time I rode, we arrived at the course at Gelsenkirchen-Horst just in time to change. The course itself is about a mile round, but the National Course is run in a complicated figure of eight within this and one seems to go round and round in circles innumerable times. The owners of the horse I was to ride wanted him ridden from in front, but no way would I have found my way round the course, so I had to remain in the pack until Tim said, 'a circuit to go' when I tried, unsuccessfully, to take the lead. I also had a trip down to the South of France to ride at Cagnes-sur-Mer.

I won my second Amateur Riders Championship that season; in fact for all practical purposes it had been decided by the end of April and with the continued support of John Jenkins, I just ticked over on his firm ground horses.

I had discussed my future with The Jockey Club, who had threatened to restrict me to only fifty rides a season against professionals if I carried on as an amateur. Both Oliver and John Jenkins had promised me rides on their horses. It was a chance I couldn't afford to turn down and I was also well aware of the possibility of picking up a few of F.T. Winter's rides.

Funds as an amateur also had a large bearing on my decision to turn professional. It is a myth to suppose that amateurs earn a fortune with back-

Mark and Sara Bradstock (nee Lawrence) with whom I shared a cottage at Lambourn.

handers and presents; while I was riding I can assure any doubting Thomas that that was not the case. So the possibility of earning a regular income, as a professional jockey, made the potential change in my status very appealing. As an amateur I earned a small wage as a pupil or assistant trainer, little more than a stable lad's wage. My expenses had to be funded out of this or with financial help from father. I generally relied on lifts to and from the races; Steve Smith-Eccles was particularly helpful in my early days at Newmarket, as he was the only National Hunt Jockey there, and we became very close friends. Otherwise, to drive yourself to Worcester from Newmarket would cost you £30.00 or so in petrol, plus the wear and tear on the car, add another £5.00 for the valet. All this added up alarmingly if you were getting 100 or more rides in a season. Finances became a bit better during my last season, when I was at Lambourn, as there were many more lifts available, and most of the National Hunt courses I was riding at are closer to Lambourn than Newmarket.

My decision to wait until ten days before the season started to apply

Herbie a few weeks old at Newmarket.

Me, in my Newmarket amateur days, and Herbie asleep in Oliver's house.

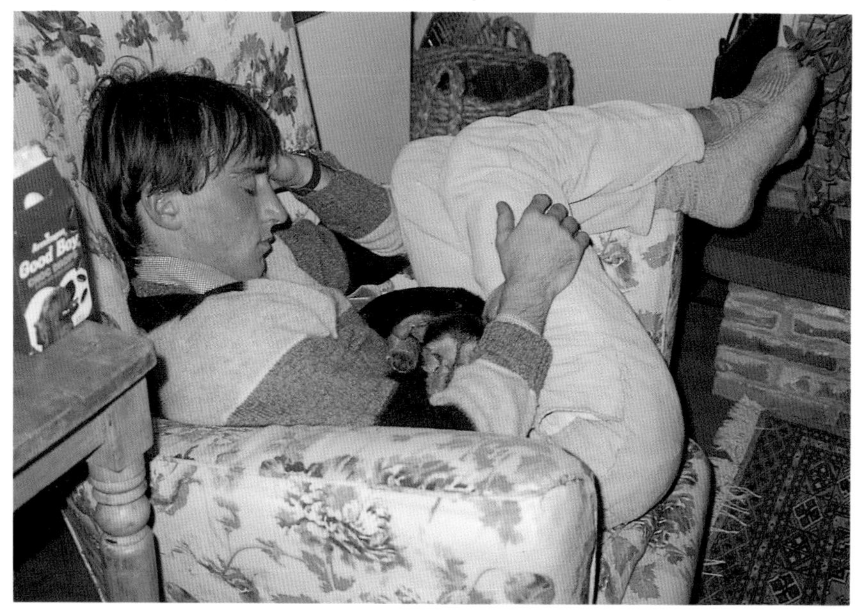

for my licence can be attributed in no small part to my conscience. I was once again letting father down regarding the farm, but any reticence father might have shown was soon dispelled by Fred Winter who told him, 'Don't waste his time insisting he goes farming, he should be a jockey.' Any misgivings I might have had were soon put to the back of my mind when father showed, as he always has done, total support for my new career.

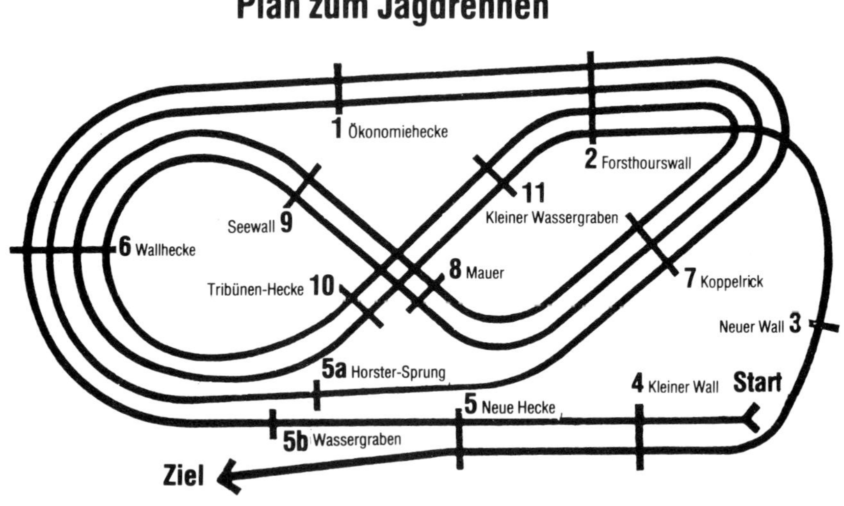

Diagonal-Bahn ca. 6800m

4, 5, 5b, 6, 1, 2, 7, 5a, 6, 1, 2, 7, 8, 9, 6, 10, 11, 2, 7, 8, 9, 6, 10, 11, 2, 3, 4, 5

First Season as Professional and First Whitbread
July 1985 - June 1986

Unlike flat jockeys, the close season for jump jockeys is relatively short, in fact under eight weeks. The jump season starts in late July or early August and runs on until the beginning of June the next year. Hardly had my final season as an amateur finished than I was embarking on what is loosely called pre-season preparation. Pre-season training as an amateur consisted of one run a week and maybe twenty press-ups. The whole thing went up a gear once I'd turned professional, to two runs and forty press-ups a week. I managed to keep step mentally with my physical fitness, so that by the start of the season I was twice as prepared for my new career!

My new career got off to a good start, not due to my extensive preparations, but to John Jenkins. He had helped me to a great extent to win both my amateur titles, possibly because he had backed me, and it was his support, when I turned professional, which gave me the best imaginable start.

I certainly didn't have a surfeit of experience when I started riding for John, so it wasn't unnatural for me to make the occasional 'cock-up' in a race. He made sure he told me when I did, but that was the end of it and, all things being equal, I would still ride the horse. That sort of confidence is paramount if a trainer and jockey are to have a good working relationship; a jockey with flair wins races and you only get the flair if you have the confidence in the team behind you.

John Jenkins's yard in Epsom differed somewhat in its day-to-day running from yards in either Newmarket or Lambourn; the approach could be described as more casual, not that it affected his output of win-

My good friends John and Wendy Jenkins.

ners as John was, until Martin Pipe took over his position, the foremost trainer of fast ground horses in the country. Schooling sessions before the start of the season must have been highly entertaining for any spectator. John had a nasty habit of creeping up behind you, without you realising, and giving the three-year-old you were about to school for the first time in its life, a crack with a 'long tom' around the heels. Something that always amused him, but did nothing for my pre-season nerves. Be that as it may, John's youngsters were always well schooled and when they ran I knew they would be both fit and good jumpers.

The West Country circuit dominates National Hunt racing for the first six weeks of the season and John had a team of ten horses permanently stabled down there. Regardless of the ground, they would run at both Devon and Exeter and Newton Abbot, sometimes two or three times a week, partnered by either Steve Smith-Eccles or myself.

Eccles was very much my mentor and steered me in the right direction in all matters concerning the West Country. We stayed at the Palace Hotel, Torquay and, no matter where we went, everybody seemed to know Eccles. It was a very steady existence - tennis or golf in the morning, a quick sleep and then off to the races. After racing it was anybody's guess! I had stepped into John Francome's shoes, not as a rider, but as Eccles' changing room mate.

Simon Sherwood, the professional jockey, got off to a bad start; my first ride, Celtic Story in a novice chase at Newton Abbot, earned me £49.50 for the indignity of a fall; still it was better than falling as an amateur, for that pleasure it would have cost me somewhere in the region of £30! But Rockfield Boy at Devon and Exeter, owned by one of John's main patrons, Nick Goymer, got me off the mark and what a relief it was. Rockfield Boy was the horse who tipped up at Uttoxeter giving me bad concussion when I was chasing my first Amateur Riders Championship, so this win repaid some of that grief. Winners then began to flood in, with the assistance of horses like Wassem, Crown Land and Houston Belle. By the time we reached the Hennessy meeting at the end of November, I'd ridden forty winners and was seven winners clear of my nearest pursuer, Eccles.

A professional jockey's life encompasses far more than just riding winners. Organisation runs a close second to riding and whilst the majority of flat jockeys have agents to organise both their lives and their rides, jump jockeys, on the whole, do most of the work themselves. The advent of the cellular 'phone proved a life saver, with jockeys carrying out a lot of their work travelling to and from meetings, as well as actually at the meetings themselves. The likes of Peter Scudamore and Richard Dunwoody don't sit on a 'phone to impress, they organise their rides and schooling sessions anything up to ten days in advance.

I successfully made the transition from amateur to professional in every aspect except one - organising my rides. It was inevitable that I would finally be caught out. When asked if I could ride, my usual answer was fairly non-committal, along the lines of, 'I think it will be okay'. Philip Mitchell is renowned for telephoning jockeys well in advance to book them for rides and, in keeping with this habit, rang me asking if I would ride Billion Boy at Plumpton. My standard answer came out, cunningly designed, so I thought, to give me the necessary leeway if a better offer came up. Philip, on the other hand, took it as read, so you can imagine his displeasure when he learned I was going to ride Asticot for John Jenkins. It was another of those unfortunate situations; in my mind Billion Boy was only a provisional booking, so it was only natural that I agreed to ride John's horse. Firstly, I'd already won on Asticot and secondly, my loyalties leaned heavily towards John. Such reasoning failed to impress Philip, who insisted I rode his. It started to dawn on me there was more to all this than one ride at Plumpton; maybe I was the unfortunate pawn in the middle and acting as a scapegoat for an old grudge between the two trainers?

The plot thickened the next day in the weighing room at Plumpton when the two of them nearly came to blows, while I cowered, red- faced and very embarrassed in the changing room. Philip got his way and I rode Billion Boy, while Steve Smith-Eccles rode Asticot. I was so incensed with rage that I would have been quite pleased if Billion Boy had been beaten, but he was too good and won by five lengths! To add insult to injury, John was fined £300 by the stewards. The whole incident was much the most exciting event at Plumpton that day and it came as no surprise when it led in the next day's *The Sporting Life*. As the whole thing was instigated by my own inefficiency, I felt guilty that not only had I not been punished, but that I'd ridden a winner to boot. Still, an important lesson had been learned and from then on bookings were treated rather more seriously.

Jockeys often like to claim they are insensitive towards the horses they ride and, as Steve Smith-Eccles says, 'they are just tools of the trade'. They might say it but I know it isn't true. We all have our favourites and I have certainly seen Steve very upset when a special horse has been hurt. Favourites don't necessarily have to be the best, they just have to be characters and genuine on the racecourse.

The Breener definitely fell into this category; not only was he a lovely horse, all of us were also very aware what an important part he had played in starting off Oliver's training career. He had progressed from hurdles to fences and had won his first novice chase, the Hopeful Chase, at Newbury on 23rd November, sprinting clear of Dunkirk to win by an easy ten lengths. His next target was an Embassy qualifier at Cheltenham. If anything he lacked a little bit in guts for chasing, he was probably too intelligent for the job, but the indications suggested he would overcome that problem and, with his class, he looked destined for the very top.

The Cheltenham race was on 6th December, the Friday before the Bula Hurdle and the Still Forks Trucks Gold Cup. The day had started

Philip Mitchell.

well. Oliver ran Oppidan in the opener and we finished second to Josh Gifford's Midnight Count. It was a most encouraging second run from the ex-Irish five-year-old. I then had a great ride on the former Gold Cup winner, Brown Chamberlin, in the big chase of the day (The Food Brokers Armour Chase), finishing third, beaten only ten lengths by Run and Skip. It was a tremendous run from a horse who had been off the racecourse for twenty-one months and the stage was now set for The Breener, who had all the potential to be another Brown Chamberlin.

Cameron, the travelling head lad, led out onto the course and as he let us go to canter to the start, he wished us his customary 'good luck'.

That day it was said with just a little more feeling than usual, because The Breener was his pride and joy. But luck deserted us and The Breener did the splits on landing at the second last and went down. As he lay there, I prayed he was only winded but, after two minutes with hardly a movement, I began to fear the worst. Oliver couldn't bring himself to come the last fifty yards, preferring to watch from the rails. Cameron ran down. The poor man was in a terrible state and just lay by the horse's head, as the dreaded curtains were erected. What had started out as a good day had ended in disaster; it was as if I'd lost a close friend and I felt sick. I only lost one other horse during my riding career, which was also a very distressing experience.

Ludlow was a course I seldom enjoyed going to, not that Bob Davies, the former jockey and now Clerk of the Course, didn't prepare it immaculately, but because it was a two-and-a-half hour drive, often done on my own as Oliver would nearly always refuse to go. My sentiments hardly improved following one particularly bad day when I had three rides. It was inevitable the day would be full of drama, they always were in that part of the world, probably on account of the fact that Lucy, my girlfriend, used to live near there when she was married. It was the first time I had been there that season.

The first ride was for John Jenkins in the seller, a 9 to 1 shot fully expected to run well, but which instead refused to race. The horse had a history of this problem, so it wasn't a total surprise, but nevertheless an irritating state of affairs resulting in an automatic stewards' enquiry. They were satisfied with my explanation.

My next ride was for Mrs. Thomas on a horse which had not run that year and, as a professional jockey, I doubted my wisdom in accepting the ride. I gave it what might be called a 'very indifferent ride'. Throughout most of the race we were towards the back of the seventeen-runner field but finished rather too strongly, which was noticed. The inevitable announcement, 'stewards enquiry', once again echoed around the Shropshire hills. Once again the stewards seemed satisfied with my explanation.

I had one more chance to improve my standing with the local punters, Rich Blue in a two-mile novice hurdle race. The omens didn't look good. He was an ex-sprinter who had been sent to Ludlow in the belief he might get two miles on the tight track. He was the sort of horse who gave you a great feeling half-a-mile out, but close to home would run out of puff!!

As planned I held him up and as we turned out of the back straight, I was going as well as anything. Then, between the last two flights of hurdles, he stopped, as if he'd been shot. Once that happens there is absolutely no point on being hard on a horse - it isn't the horse's fault, he doesn't get the trip and when he is punch drunk with fatigue there is no point in knocking the living daylights out of him. It should impress no one, apart from a few misguided punters.

I say 'it should', for the simple reason that the now familiar 'stewards enquiry' once again rang out around the racecourse, much to the amusement of my fellow jockeys. My patience was beginning to run out, especially when they started to doubt my riding on Rich Blue. I was both staggered and annoyed. The slightest inference as to a jockey's honesty made by the stewards can have a pretty damning affect on his future, and in the case of Rich Blue, I thought it did nothing but fully expose the stewards who have no race-riding experience.

Don't get me wrong. I am a great believer in amateur stewards but I feel it is essential that they have race-riding experience so that they can appreciate the many foibles connected with the whole affair. All too frequently they show total inflexibility, adhere rigidly to the facts in front of them and fail to accept jockeys' explanations. It must never be forgotten that horses are not machines and, like human beings, have 'off days'. There may be no rhyme or reason, no wholly acceptable explanation, just an off day and when that happens (which it does quite a lot, if it didn't there wouldn't be any bookmakers), the stewards ought to throw the formbook out of the window and simply accept the situation.

The worst example of stewards' inflexibility happened at Newbury when I rode Wing and a Prayer for John Jenkins. He was a prolific winner and a potentially brilliant steeplechaser; the ground that day at Newbury was fairly firm and John didn't want to run, but his owner, David Steele, insisted, so John asked me to look after the horse. There might only have been six runners, but after two flights we were struggling, they were going so quickly. Wing and a Prayer was giving me no feel at all and I trailed in a well-beaten fifth, even though I was the 3 to 1 second favourite. The stewards seemed less than happy with my explanation and recorded it. Their way of saying 'we don't believe you, but we can't prove anything'. As far as I was concerned I had done the right thing, the horse was not going well and my job was to make sure that the horse wasn't permanently damaged. The next day Wing and a Prayer died of a perforated heart. Enough said.

I should say that my own experiences with the stewards were, on the whole, very good. I was never suspended or, for that matter, fined and only had a couple of my explanations 'noted'.

If a professional jockey's emotions include sadness, then anger and frustration must also be listed. There were numerous occasions when I got both very angry and very frustrated, be it with a horse, an owner, a trainer or a jockey. In any competitive environment such emotions are bound to rear their ugly head; the secret was never to show them at the time (which is easy to say sitting down, writing away but rather harder to put into practice in the heat of the moment).

Similar emotions are shared by the punter, although he differs in one respect, as he tends to be somewhat more expansive, airing his views immediately. Two Arthur Daley look-alikes illustrate my point - Houston Belle, trained by John Jenkins and owned by Robert Ellis, was beaten when an 11 to 10 on chance at Ascot. We anticipated a race run with no gallop, so changed the riding tactics to take this into account. We were wrong and finished third, beaten seventeen lengths. As we returned to the unsaddling enclosure, the two Daley look-alikes appeared, definitely set on a collision course, venting their views; there was no mistaking their feelings. I began to feel singularly uncomfortable on top of Houston Belle and, if one of them had had his way, I would have been off the horse pretty quickly. Help came in the form of one of the 'bowler-hatted' gentlemen who averted what might have been a fairly unpleasant scene. I must confess to not being a great fan of the bowler-hatted fraternity at Ascot; they seem over-impressed with their own importance, swaying towards unhelpfulness rather than helpfulness but, on that particular occasion, I was very glad of their existence.

The weather took a turn for the worse after Christmas and the Lambourn Valley was covered by five inches of snow. As long as it doesn't last for too long, a break in the middle of the season is gratefully received by most parties involved with jump racing. With a season that lasts for ten months, there can be no better tonic than a few days away to get you through the rest of it and, with that in mind, Kim Bailey organised a trip to Val d'Isere. Hearing about it I managed to squeeze myself onto 'Bailey Tours' twelve hours before they left.

Most casual observers would have concluded I was skiing for the first time. For three days I was nothing more than a pest on the French slopes, with a penchant for causing mayhem on the 'T-Bar' lifts. Arranging myself comfortably at the departure point of the T-Bar for another long haul up the mountain, I slipped on a particularly icy surface and immediately saw what I was looking for - a pole sticking out of the snow, with a mushroom-like top, placed with people like myself in mind, so that we might grab it and save ourselves. I did exactly that. Not only did I fail to save myself, the T-Bar ground to a halt - I had grabbed the emergency brake. A T-Bar stopped on the side of the mountain is not good, especially if you are on a down slope, and there they were, hundreds of them up the mountain, stranded like beached whales.

After that debacle, I promised myself I would avoid the T-Bar at all costs. By the third day I'd grasped the basics of skiing. I could sort of stand up and go in a straight line. I got off to a particularly good start on one run and in no time must have been going as fast as Franz Klammer in his heyday. The thrill was quickly overtaken by horror - I was aiming straight for the T-Bar and there was nothing I could do about it. I was going far too fast to fall over. Suddenly it dawned on the T-Bar users that something faster than Franz Klammer in his heyday was about to slice them in half. Terrified Frenchmen leapt for safety, others fell, out of sheer fright while I, the mad Englishman, flew past them. It was then I decided that the quicker we got a 'phone call telling us racing was about to resume the better. Luckily the call didn't come for a few days and by then, heavily disguised I hasten to add, I had become sufficiently proficient to do what I liked, when I liked, without endangering other people.

Once racing started again, the Jockeys Championship began to slip away from me. Peter Scudamore was beginning to assert his professionalism and experience and my main source of winners, John Jenkins, had temporarily dried up with only ten winners coming from January onwards. Oliver's horses, on the other hand, continued to run out of their skins and he ended his second season with forty-eight winners.

That is not to say that the second half of my season was without its excitements. The horses in Fred Winter's yard at Uplands were not running quite as well as expected. Various opinions were expressed, notably the retirement of John Francome and, consequently, Ben de Haan and Jimmy Duggan bore the brunt of it. Some of the owners were asking for someone else and Fred Winter was in a no-win situation.

When John Francome announced his retirement the previous season, Mr. Winter had a word with my brother, Oliver, about my availability to ride a few for him. Mr. Winter now called me into his office to, in his own words, 'discuss something'. He sat behind his desk, looking at me with those steely eyes I remembered so well from the first time I ever rode out for him. I had ridden a few for him earlier in the season, not least Brown Chamberlin, but was at a loss as to why he'd called me in. He certainly made me suffer. He had a habit of sitting and staring at you, with the face that bore all the hallmarks of achievement. Now he looked me up and down, inspecting me. He then asked me to ride some of his horses. As a result I was lucky enough to ride some of the best horses in the country, not least Fifty Dollars More and Half Free. The ride on Half Free in the Cathcart Cup, the 'getting out stakes' on the last day of the Cheltenham Festival, although virtually unnoticed by the Festival crowd, was a great thrill. I knew Half Free's invincible record around Cheltenham and that the little horse would be going best at certain areas on the track. True to form he tore up the hill to beat The Mighty Mac and Western Sunset, for my first professional Festival winner.

Jumping the last on Plundering to win the 1986 Whitbread.

Very happy after the Whitbread. (See frontispiece for Her Majesty The Queen Mother presenting prizes).

Liverpool gave me a winner on Fifty Dollars More and a fall on Plundering in the Grand National for Mrs. Miles Valentine at the Canal Turn first time. A stupid mistake by me caused our departure, which gave our followers some disappointment as Plundering was a 25 to 1 shot. Trying to make up a little ground, I ventured to jump the Canal Turn on the tight inside but was crossed by a loose horse.

It was not until the Whitbread at Sandown in May that I was able to produce the just rewards for such an opportunity. The race for the Trainers Title was close. Nicky Henderson led, but if Fred Winter won the Whitbread there would be little to choose between the two of them. Therefore, not unnaturally, Winter went to the race triple-handed - I Haventalight, Dumper and Plundering.

I was hoping to ride I Haventalight, but instead was asked to ride Plundering for Mrs. Miles Valentine. I owed his followers something, having fallen in the National and, as luck would have it, at the end of yet another memorable Whitbread, Plundering and I emerged as the winners. Any regrets I had about not winning the Jockeys Championship were quickly forgotten. As I received my trophy from The Queen Mother, I knew I'd won one of the most prestigious handicaps in the calendar.

It was, however, an obvious disappointment not to win the Championship, when you knew that with a bit of luck and good fortune it might have been yours. I ended the season in second place, with seventy-nine winners, twelve behind Peter Scudamore.

Two days after the season ended a team of jockeys left for Australia. It consisted of Peter Scudamore (Captain), Hwyel Davies, Steve Smith-Eccles and myself. Twenty-four hours later we arrived in Melbourne, only to find we had been booked into a motel which would have suited Compo from 'Last of the Summer Wine' right down to the ground. Eccles isn't used to staying in motels and immediately complained, something he always does. (I put it down to his size and the natural inferiority complex it brings about.) The complaints worked. The Southern Cross, a five-star hotel, was a great improvement!

The series was a big success and an experience - neither the horses nor the courses were anything very special, but there is always something to be learned from riding in a foreign country. For instance, at one course we learned that Hywel, riding the expected favourite, was in for a rough ride. Armed with that information, Captain Peter gave me strict instructions to protect him, something I did admirably, although I say so myself, until I fell off and broke my collar-bone; so much for protecting Hywel!

The Australians did all they could to make the trip a success and I would no doubt be able to tell you far more about them if it hadn't been for Eccles's jacket. He insisted on wearing a very dodgy, loud, striped, double-breasted jacket wherever we went in the evening. The Australians were not altogether familiar with such jackets; the sight of someone turning up looking like a cross between a cornetto salesman and a pimp did little for the men on the door, who would err on the side of caution and send us on our way, assuming we must be gay.

Second Season as Professional - Enter Desert Orchid

July 1986 - June 1987

There was plenty to do after getting back from the Australian trip, not least moving house. Having joined the paid ranks I took the unprecedented step of buying a house, something that might have been slightly unnerving at the time but was to prove to be much my shrewdest financial move, as house prices in the area never stop going up, regardless of the state of the economy.

Willowend is an ideal cottage for me, cosy but with plenty of light, three bedrooms, and a garden that isn't too big, with a stream running along the edge of it. Like Baytree Cottage, Willowend isn't in Lambourn but in Eastbury, another small village, full of friends involved in racing and just that little bit nearer to Lambourn along the valley road. It doesn't matter how far you are moving house, the whole thing is an ordeal but I was lucky enough to have the help of my girlfriend, Lucy, whose role was crucial - not only did she stop me boiling over, her knowledge of interior design proved invaluable when it came to decorating the place.

After the move the two of us went on holiday to Val de Lobo, with Eccles, Di Haine, and John and Miriam Francome. It was a much needed break. The house move had taken every bit as much out of me as I had expected and there was a need for some sun. Outsiders tend to criticize jockeys for going on this holiday and that holiday, but what they forget is that a jockey's life is a high-pressure existence. During a season jockeys drive around 40,000 miles, race six days a week on good, bad, slow and indifferent jumpers, and if you don't get away when the opportunity presents itself, you quickly go mad.

The holiday went a long way to re-charging my batteries but I had my doubts about the coming season. I no longer had the assistance of John Jenkins, who had taken the view that he wanted a jockey on a more permanent basis, and had therefore snapped up John White. My doubts weren't in any way lessened when I went up to Market Rasen on the 18th August, 1986, (not a short trip from Lambourn!) with Lucy, only to break my scapula, resulting in a two-week lay-off. Not a distinguished start to the season.

The first three months of the season produced little of any note; Timlyn, a dear horse of Toby Baldings helped me tick along, increasing my tally by four.

Glen International, owned by the intrepid punter Terry Ramsden, sponsored a North versus South Jockeys' competition. The competition proved to be an unmitigated success with both the jockeys and the sponsors. It received plenty of media coverage, no doubt helped by the fact it was the first of its kind, and clearly demonstrated that the opportunities for sponsorship are considerable. The lack of enterprise shown by com-

Willowend, my cottage in Eastbury.

On holiday in Portugal with Steve Smith-Eccles.

mercial organisations regarding sponsorship in the racing industry always surprises me. Let's face it, racing is a part of the entertainment industry and by the very nature of it happening six days a week, every week of the year, its media profile is very high. But when it comes to sponsorship, it lags a long way behind its fellow sports. Of course it is not just a lack of resourcefulness on the part of sponsors or potential sponsors; much of the blame can be attributed to The Jockey Club. So much is interwoven by a web of petty bureaucracy, coupled to a reluctance to come to terms with the modern world. Only very recently has corporate entertainment found a footing in racing, with hospitality villages at such meetings as the National Hunt Festival at Cheltenham in March, and the Grand National at Aintree the following month. Obviously, they are prestige meetings, worthy of tented villages, but the scope at the smaller meetings is considerable. Racecourses ought to be far more willing to provide hospitality boxes at competitive prices and not the exorbitant rates we are used to seeing.

The possibility of 'quick lease ownership' ought to become readily available, so that companies, or even individuals for that matter, can entertain their clients with the added thrill of watching a horse run in their name. At present, the best anyone can hope for is a top jockey or trainer to come to their tent or box, either before or after racing, and give a talk.

The Jockey Club, when it wants, can work wonders. For instance, it seems to have managed to stamp out the terrible habit of 'nobbling' horses (doping them to slow them) which is particularly dangerous for both horse and jockey over fences. All the time I was riding I don't think I ever heard of a horse being 'nobbled' which must be an absolute nightmare for any jockey. Another example of where The Jockey Club has been extremely effective and forward-thinking is the revival of Liverpool and the saving of the Grand National. Much of the good work there has been done by two ex-amateur Champion Riders, Chris Collins and Peter Greenall. Everybody has pulled together, The Jockey Club, the Aintree Racecourse Authorities and the major sponsors, Seagram (the International drinks giants) to great effect and the meeting goes from strength to strength every year.

As a former jockey, it is not my intention to suggest the jump jockeys' lot is a miserable one. All I'm saying is that compared to other top sportsmen, a top jump jockey's income pales into insignificance. Granted, the immediate financial rewards are far less than other top sports, but the main reason is the jockey's inability to sponsor a product while he is riding. I appreciate the practical difficulties of sponsoring a product when wearing colours, but the French have overcome the problem by allowing commercial sponsorship on a sash across the colours. The very thought of advertising a product on the seams of your breeches, as John Francome tried to do, very nearly brought about an end to The Jockey Club as we know it, such was their consternation, so the thought of sashes advertising the likes of 'Coca Cola' are obviously way beyond the realms of possibility!

'The ups and downs of racing', is a rather banal remark heard daily on the racecourse, but still very true. The season was ticking along, nothing had happened to set the world alight, then suddenly it went mad with the Christmas meeting at Kempton. Obviously the highlight of the meeting was Desert Orchid's win in the King George (fully described in the first chapter of this book), but other winners came in abundance. Also on the Boxing Day, Agathist won a valuable three-year-old hurdle for Gavin

David Elsworth.

Pritchard-Gordon and the next day Stirabout got me off to a good start winning a novice chase. The West Awake set off on his ascent to the top by winning comfortably and the scene looked set for a treble, with Drive On Jimmy, bought by David Bott to replace The Breener, fully expected to win.

Drive On Jimmy hit the first fence down the back and pecked on landing - I flew over his head, but very stupidly got my arm caught in the breast plate. The breast plate is designed to go around a horse's neck and not have arms in it. Drive On Jimmy, having eyed me up with some suspicion, quite rightly tried to get up. I discovered arms caught in breast plates don't easily come out and, as he tried to get up, I dragged him back down on top of me. He then, fortunately, managed to free himself, leaving me lying in immense pain; I had broken my back but there was no displacement. In a matter of minutes life had taken a dramatic U-turn: suddenly I was faced with four weeks off. Still, in situations like that, the secret is to make the best of a bad job so with that in mind, Lucy and I went off for a holiday in the Canary Islands.

At the risk of stating the obvious, falls are an inherent part of the job and generally are the cause of far more concern to close friends and family than the jockeys themselves. The reason is twofold - firstly, a jockey worried about falling has lost his bottle and secondly, you, as the jockey, are far more aware what has happened, having fallen, than the people in the stand. I was never in a hurry to get to my feet. I would simply lie there and carry out a human M.O.T. on myself - wiggling my toes, fingers and wrists in turn to check everything was in working order.

The fact that it took a few seconds proved all too much for my mother, who would agonize in the stands, waiting for me to stand up. To put her mind at rest we devised a simple code - I would raise an arm if all was well. Mother was much happier, the code worked, but one day not in my interests. I fell at the furthest fence from the stands; I was fine but on those occasions it's best to feel a bit winded, so that when the ambulance comes round with the doctor you get a lift back to the weighing room, saving yourself the walk. My arm raising, by some quirk of bad luck, coincided with the doctor's enquiry as to my well being. Satisfied my raised arm was in response to his question, off went the ambulance, leaving me with a twenty-minute walk back to the weighing room.

One of my first victories after my enforced holiday came at Windsor in February. Any aspirations to a knighthood or some similar decoration, not that I had any, were certainly not improved that day. One of the television channels was doing a programme on 'The Queen Mother and Her Racehorses'. They had been to Lambourn and filmed the horses on the downs and at her trainer's, Fulke Walwyn. It was then to Windsor where they hoped to film a Royal winner. The racing public were also hoping they filmed a Royal winner for they sent the Queen Mother's horse, Sun Rising, off 13 to 8 favourite. The Sherwood camp ran Numerate, who wasn't the subject of any media coverage, second favourite at 100 to 30.

Either Numerate is a very bad sport, or no one told him the film crew were filming Sun Rising and not him. Whatever it was, he behaved

The presentation of the trophies after the 1986 King George VI Chase. (I've already changed out of Desert Orchid's blue and grey colours to ride in the next race.)

in an extraordinary way - everyone, not least The Queen Mother, could not have been happier with the way the plot was developing. This film had all the makings of the perfect fairy-tale ending. Sun Rising was going to win as they approached the final two fences. Then it happened - Numerate spotted a camera that was obviously not an R.T.S. camera. Out of charity I'll say vanity was behind his motive; anyway, he sprouted wings and got up to beat Sun Rising by half a length. You know, you can't win at this game, the general attitude of the Windsor racegoers was not all that dissimilar to the Ludlow racegoers in the previous season.

8th February was my first visit to ride in Ireland. Barnbrook Again ran in the Wessel Cable Champion Hurdle, at Leopardstown, and he was a hot favourite at 5 to 4 on. The race was a disaster; we were beaten two lengths by Deep Idol. Arguably I was caught looking over the wrong shoulder, but agreed to disagree. Peter Scuadmore also came out to ride Thelastofthebrownies, a heavily-backed horse in the next race. I went to watch the race from one of the bars and got very excited when it appeared that Peter had the race in his pocket. Turning into the straight he seemed to make up twenty lengths over the rest of the field as they all swung very wide. It soon became apparent that Peter had taken the wrong course. If it hadn't been for Eddie Harty, who helped to smuggle us out of the chang-

Brian Delaney, formerly head lad to F.T. Winter, now for Charlie Brooks.

Chris Clarke, Oliver's head lad.

ing room, I dare say both of us could still well be there, impaled on some fence!

The other major highlight of the season was the Festival at Cheltenham. It was fast becoming a lucky meeting for me and that year proved no exception. The West Awake's victory in the Sun Alliance Hurdle was cause for great celebrations, for it was not only Oliver's first Festival winner as a trainer, it was also the first Festival winner for Christopher and Maggie Heath, who were to become not just Oliver's biggest owners but very nearly the biggest National Hunt owners in racing at present. I also had a memorable ride on Barnbrook Again, finishing third in the Champion Hurdle, beaten by See You Then and the American challenger, Flatterer.

The Liverpool meeting came around again in early April and the usual team of Charlie Brooks (who has now taken over Fred Winter's yard), Mark Bradstock and Charles Egerton, the bloodstock agent to mention but a few of the more obvious, stayed at the Adelphi Hotel. The meeting was very productive with Aldino storming away with the Glenlivet Hurdle and The West Awake completing an unique Cheltenham/Liverpool double. I didn't accept a ride in the National. I am a great believer in not taking a ride in that particular race unless you have a horse with a genuinely good chance. Instead I had a very relaxed time in the changing room with the valets at the expense of the other jockeys.

When there are only four weeks left of the season and your position is fairly secure in the Jockeys Table, the enthusiasm to ride a headstrong and sweaty individual for John Jenkins starts to wane. John knew I was going to Huntingdon for Oliver, he asked if I would ride one. Out of loyal-

Rhonehurst - Oliver's house and yard at Lambourn..

Aldino winning at Liverpool - I was also to win the Scottish Champion Hurdle on him at Ayr in 1989.

ty I stupidly agreed but ten miles short of Huntingdon on the A1, I wasn't so sure. Oliver pulled into a garage and I rang John, saying I couldn't make it because of the traffic. I did such a good job that I convinced myself we had been caught in the traffic and feeling very pleased with myself I expected John to say, 'O.K.'. Not a bit of it. Laughing he said, 'make sure you are on time, you shouldn't have any difficulty, I've just passed you in the garage'. I fell and split my lip.

I ended my second professional season having fared quite well, finishing fourth in the table with sixty-four winners which, all things considered, wasn't bad, taking into account the lack of John Jenkins's ammunition and the time I'd spent off due to injury. I must admit, I was glad when it ended although sadly my final memory of the season left a slightly sour taste in the mouth.

Carroll Gray had a terrible fall at Stratford and was lying prostrate across the landing side of the fence. There were about twenty of us in the race and the next time round he was still there and there was only room for about two horses to jump upsides. Chaos took over with the result that four of us fell. Carroll still lay there, attended by a very brave nurse and, to save the situation from escalating, Mark Perrett and I decided to take some positive action. We stood twenty yards apart, in front of the fence, directing the field around it. In circumstances such as that only the doctor can order the field to miss the fence. The outcome of the race - void.

Third Season as Professional and Second Whitbread
July 1987 - June 1988

When I turned professional I anticipated riding for a couple of seasons, by which time I would be both fed up with the sight of horses and the sight of motorways. Extraordinary though it may sound, this very point played an important part in my decision to turn professional. When you 'hang up your boots' as a professional, you do so in the full knowledge that it is final.

One of my fears as an amateur was the thought of going back to Essex and point-to-pointing *ad infinitum* until either the supply of whisky ran out or the saddlers complained they couldn't make reins to accommodate my ever-increasing backward seat any longer. At least I knew that when I gave up as a professional, my career as a jockey would have come to an end.

I was right in one respect. I was fed up with the sight of motorways, but not of the sight of horses. After the now customary fortnight in Val de Lobo with the usual team, we were off again at the start of the 1987/88 season. I started the season with a little more clout than previously. I had managed to get some sponsorship with the large firm of stockbrokers, James Capel Global Investments, through one of their directors, John Green who was also one of John Jenkins's owners.

In return for some sponsorship, aimed at my car and travelling expenses, I was expected to do some public relations work by wearing James Capel clothes and talking to their clients at the races. It was a relaxed arrangement which worked extremely well; generally John would ring up a couple of days before a London meeting and ask me to go to a certain box before racing. I would then talk to their clients, who tended to be Americans, before racing and then, after racing, would bring back a few of the other jockeys to talk to them. Not very daunting stuff.

The Hennessy meeting threw a totally new light on the whole thing. James Capel had a marquee, over 200 guests and a rostrum which I quickly discovered was for me to stand on and deliver a talk full of substance. I treat public speaking in the same manner that I treat a visit to the bank manager - plenty of preparation, know exactly what you are going to say and keep it to the minimum. This was an altogether new experience and one I didn't relish, not that I had much time to think about it! I have absolutely no idea what I said, or how I said it, but if past performances are anything to go by, it wouldn't have been very good.

My previous public speaking duties had been confined exclusively to the Bollinger Dinner, held annually in London for the National Hunt Awards. One of the drawbacks of winning either the amateur or the professional rider's title is the requirement to give a speech at the dinner, thereby ruining any chance you might have of enjoying it. Two amateur titles meant two speeches, neither of which were made any easier by John Francome winning the professional title and speaking before me. John has the marvellous gift of being able to stand up and deliver a speech, full of wit and anecdotes, in his Wiltshire drawl without the assistance of any aids. The only gift I had was the gift to panic before I gave a speech, heightened once when I somewhat proudly told Lord Oaksey the gist of what I was going to say. His reaction wasn't favourable. He told me I couldn't possibly say what I wanted to and that I had to think again. Not what you want to hear ten minutes before you are expected to stand up.

On the racing front, I had a nice early winner at Worcester on 8th August and I started to get the impression quite early in the season that I could be in for a vintage year, quality being the order of the day, rather than quantity. I was beginning to forge quite a partnership with David Elsworth and was eagerly awaiting the reappearance of Barnbrook Again. Following his third in the Champion Hurdle the previous season, David decided to send him chasing and he eventually made his debut over the larger obstacles at Devon and Exeter on 10th November. There was no mistaking the quality of his performance - he might not have had a lot to beat but he jumped impeccably and won by a distance.

Barnbrook Again's next race was even more impressive, when he beat another useful performer, Prideaux Boy, by twenty lengths in a canter in the Hurst Park Chase at Ascot on 20th November. I might have won a King George on Desert Orchid but at that time there was something very special about the feeling Barnbrook Again gave me. It was an exhibition of class that totally enraptured me and as I returned to the winner's enclosure at Ascot I felt that this performance was the best I had ever experienced from a novice.

Barnbrook's ability to totally outclass his rivals in a race can be put down to his cruising speed. He is one of a fortunate handful which cruise that bit quicker than the rest - it is a supreme quality in a horse as not only does it saves energy, it also ensures that most of the time the rest of the field are galloped off their feet. Add to this his ability to jump fast and well and you have the nearest thing you can get to an equine machine.

In the Hennessy Gold Cup at Newbury on the 28th November, I had a good ride on Durham Edition for Arthur Stephenson and in the next I was second on The West Awake. He was my other equine machine in the making. As far as I was concerned he was destined right for the top of the

Barnbrook Again winning at the 1989 National Hunt Festival at Cheltenham.

three-mile chasers' ladder. He shared many of the same qualities as Barnbrook Again, but whereas Barnbrook was destined to be a two-mile type horse, The West Awake's future definitely lay in the world of staying chases. His main attribute is his attitude - he is a very relaxed horse, sometimes too relaxed, who just switches off in a race but then, when you ask him, has an amazing turn of foot for about a furlong which tends to be way beyond the capabilities of his rivals.

Boxing Day saw arguably the fastest King George VI ever to be run at Kempton. Certainly the first mile was run at breakneck speed and the pundits said the time was more appropriate to the Two Thousand Guineas than a three-mile chase. Desert Orchid (ridden by Colin Brown), Beau Ranger and Cybrandian must have been twenty lengths clear of the rest of us, going to the second fence. I was on Bolands Cross for Nick Gaselee the horse which had acted as a buffer for Dessie and me the previous year in the race. No way could Bolands Cross lay up. I ended up asking for too big a one at a fence, in the vain hope of trying to keep in touch, but unfortunately we fell and I did end up on the Sunbury turf, something which I had feared the previous year.

Nupsala, trained in France by Francais Doumen, won in convincing style, as sadly Dessie got tired over the last few fences. Nupsala's win did nothing for me, but it certainly pleased Oliver as he had been staying with him for a few days before the race. I ended up with one winner during the two-day meeting but, slightly annoyingly, also with four seconds.

The Newbury meeting in early January caused a few hiccoughs for the Sherwood Brothers' Racing Stables. Oliver, having ridden himself, can appreciate that races do not necessarily go according to plan and even the best laid out scheme can easily go adrift under National Hunt Rules.

On Saturday, 2nd January, Kodiak Island, an ex-Irish horse, was very well fancied to win the Phillip Cornes' Qualifier at Newbury and started at 6 to 4 favourite. Newbury was a course I always enjoyed riding around more than any other, including even Cheltenham. It has wonderful facilities, good horses and a lovely galloping track with plenty of room. John Francome used to ride it to perfection and I remember him telling me never to really get into a race until coming to the third last fence or flight. So, on this particular occasion, I had Kodiak Island upside at the third last flight but came up against a horse called Glide On who well and truly stuffed us by eight lengths, although I finished fifteen lengths clear of the third horse.

A recent photograph - Oliver to the right, me to the left. I put forward the theory in Chapter Two that I was twice as clever as Oliver because I had two 'A' levels to his one. I leave it to the reader to decide who is the most photogenic!

As I returned to the unsaddling enclosure, in front of the weighing room, obviously disappointed having been beaten on a 6 to 4 favourite, I was greeted by a rather miffed brother. When Oliver stands two strides back from the horse and tends to look at the horse rather than you, while you try to explain what happened, you can sense that he is not very happy. Poor Christopher and Maggie Heath, quite happy but realising a potential battle was about to start, kept quiet as Oliver opened up his barrage.

'Why did you not force it more, really you should have won'. Am I hearing this right, I thought, but anger overtook me and, apologising to Christopher and Maggie, I strode off, remarking to John Oaksey, 'I think Oliver has just joined the league of ignorant trainers'. Luckily twenty-four hours later the whole incident had been forgotten about. I think this is the only public argument we have ever had.

Oliver was fortunate enough to have a yard full of young stars who were just beginning to come to themselves, so you can imagine my anger and disappointment when the 'annual break' came in January. Statistics say a jump jockey will have a fall once in every ten rides. I have never bothered to work out how I fared against the average, but suspect I might have been on the right side for falls, but can't believe I was on the right side of the averages for breaks!

That year's break came at Newbury on the second day of the meeting, (Monday, 4th January) from Gurteen Wood, trained by Oliver and owned by the Heaths. He was the 11 to 8 favourite but we fell at the third, breaking my ankle and once again I was compelled to have a mid-season break, this time for six weeks.

I was frequently accused, more half-heartedly than seriously, of not being terribly hungry and not taking many outside rides. Of course, there was an element of truth in the remark. I couldn't see the point of riding potentially dangerous horses which I didn't know when I was attached to a yard full of good horses and also rode a number of good horses for other trainers. When your livelihood can be put at risk through riding one 'bad 'un', I adopted the philosophy of only riding horses attached to the yards I rode for, and had therefore schooled, or horses with a proven track record.

Finances also influenced my decision. There seemed little point in driving 100 miles to a meeting and back again, which must have cost me £30 or £40 in petrol, plus wear and tear on my car. I would also have to pay my valet, just for one ride, and the end result would probably only gross me £50. Unless, that is, one was likely to ride a winner and therefore get a percentage of the first prize money.

Schooling at Rhonehurst was a job I always enjoyed and could never get bored with. Things were very different when I went down to John Jenkins - the majority of the horses I schooled at Epsom were three-year-olds, fresh off the flat and normally singularly unimpressed with the sight of a hurdle. They would duck and dive and, remembering the old saying, 'ride long, live long', down would come the stirrups, making me look like a stand-in for John Wayne.

But horses are not quite as stupid as people make them out to be and after a couple of times up the hurdles they would get the hang of things and really start to attack them. At Oliver's the horses had generally been loose-schooled before going up to the schooling grounds on Mandown. On the whole schooling with Oliver went well, everybody knew exactly what they were doing and the horses would arrive relaxed and ready to get on with the job.

Only once can I remember some dissent on my part. I was schooling an enormous horse called Five Lamps, who had been tried over fences before, but had patently failed to grasp the intricacies of jumping and was being given another chance by Oliver. He was a nine-year-old and there seemed little hope of converting him into a chaser but, as the dutiful younger brother, I agreed to have a go. Luckily he met everything on a stride first time up and jumped well. We should have stopped there and then. Next time up he jumped the first two alright, but totally 'missed' the third and broke the fence in half. The penny never dropped and the next time up, it was the turn of the first - he managed to break that as well. That was it; I pulled him up and told Oliver I was going home!

Watching all this in horror was Eddie Fisher, head gallops man and a legendary figure in Lambourn. If I had to name ten men not to get on the wrong side of, Eddie would be one of them. His gallops are his pride and joy and as long as you do what you are told, then he is a great ally and might well open a special piece of ground for you, if you have a horse running in a big race. Take him for granted, or use a piece of ground that is closed and he'll change instantly into one of the most frightening sights on earth. I can assure you, being chased by Eddie with his pitchfork is about as appealing a prospect as going into a boxing ring with Mike Tyson! Fortunately, fence breaking isn't categorized by Eddie as a reason for a bit of pitchfork throwing, so Oliver was able to walk off the gallops unscathed.

Such occasions were indeed very rare (fence breaking, not pitchfork throwing) and as a rule Oliver's horses were well mannered and only a few ever made it onto my blacklist of 'horses not to school'. Such individuals then enjoyed the tender handling of either Mark Richards or Clive Cox, who are both extremely good schooling jockeys, not to mention race jockeys. It made a lot of difference to have two other jockeys in the yard to school with. While I appreciate young, up-and-coming jockeys have to be given every opportunity to school, the principal reason for schooling is to educate horses and clearly that will always be best achieved if they are ridden by experienced jockeys. I can't remember ever going to the races doubting the ability of any of Oliver's horses to do their job.

The set-up at Rhonehurst is immaculate; the yard and the facilities are unquestionably the best in Lambourn. Oliver has the perfect approach of being relaxed but at the same time efficient. He is backed up by an exceptional head lad in Chris Clarke and supported by a very good staff. Chris is in the top echelon of head lads, having worked for both Fred Winter and Captain Head, and is wholly devoted to his horses. If anything he is too devoted and at times worries more than the situation warrants, but I suppose if he didn't behave like that his attention to detail wouldn't be what it is.

I got into the terrible habit of turning up two minutes before we pulled out. Every day I was greeted by the same sight of Chris 'walking his box', wondering if I was going to make it. As I drove into the yard I could see him thinking, 'you lazy little shit'. Probably it showed the worst side of me, but I used to glean considerable pleasure from watching him fret as I arrived.

One of the joys of Rhonehurst was the time the young horses were given to come to themselves, they were never forced, an attribute Oliver had picked up from Fred Winter. On the other hand, the same cannot be said about birthdays at Rhonehurst; the lads considered they had *carte blanche* to do what they wanted with the poor individual. Fully aware of this I parked my car close to the house on my birthday and feeling a conspiracy was afoot, I thought it prudent to remain in the safety of Oliver's house for as long as possible after breakfast.

I walked calmly towards my car, the scene had all the makings of a Clint Eastwood film; there was a eerie quiet around the yard and I felt several pairs of eyes focused on me. Not being so cool as Clint I quickened my pace and then six lads appeared from nowhere. I sprinted for the car but, to my horror, it was locked. Having your jodhpurs removed, greased and sprayed with a hose in the middle of winter is definitely not recommended.

My ankle had fully recovered by the time Cheltenham arrived. The West Awake continued to improve and impress at home and justified everyone's hopes by winning the Sun Alliance Novices' Chase over three miles. I always thought that was nearly a Gold Cup performance. Oliver's handling of The West Awake was, in a word, exemplary - never have I ridden a horse who felt so mentally and physically fit on the day. Just to put the icing on the cake, Oliver once again won the Sun Alliance Hurdle with another ex-Arthur Moore inmate, Rebel Song, giving the Sherwoods/Heaths a Festival double on the second day and enabling me to win the Ritz Jockeys Trophy for the meeting.

Fortunately by coming second on Cavvies Clown in the Gold Cup, my first ride in the big race, I managed to beat Richard Dunwoody for the Ritz Trophy. I had a great ride on Cavvies Clown, a dear little horse with very large ears. I did not realise his smallness until legged-up in the paddock. He slouched round the paddock on a loose rein, totally unflapped by the big event. In the race he jumped for fun and coming down the hill I thought we would win. Going to the second last I sensed Charter Party and Richard Dunwoody upsides, going very well, so I ended up firing Cavvies Clown at the fence, which was a mistake. He put down but somehow stayed on his feet with my reins flying up his neck and being stopped by his large ears; we both tried our hardest to get back on terms with Charter Party, but ended up a credible second.

Extraordinarily enough, that Cheltenham was responsible for one event which was subsequently to totally dominate my riding career. Colin Brown announced his retirement. It was a sad occasion as not only is Colin a dear friend, he was also a great character in the changing room. However it did open up the possibility of riding Desert Orchid, something which I have to admit, raced through my mind.

David Elsworth, in his typically cool way, mentioned in passing that if I had nothing to ride in the Martell at Liverpool I could ride Desert Orchid and then muttered something about the Whitbread. In a game of tit-for-tat I casually answered, 'Alright'.

'Alright' was not the word, there was nothing casual about me - I was overcome with excitement. However, my enthusiasm was tempered by the thought of Liverpool being left-handed. We had all been indoctrinated

Dessie and I lead the field over the water jump at Liverpool. This fence is also jumped in the Grand National course.

4

with the belief that Desert Orchid couldn't act on a left-handed course; I thought, 'I must be prepared to be shot down in flames if he fails'.

The field at Liverpool was small, I had only four rivals - Weather The Storm, Kildimo, Beau Ranger and Contradeal. The gods were on my side, Beau Ranger, the nigger in the woodpile, lost a shoe at the start and was withdrawn. With no one taking on the grey I was able to win comfortably, although it must be said he jumped slightly to the right.

Faraway Lad had pulled off a coup in the Seagram 100 Pipers Top Novices Hurdle, beating Sea Island and Ryde Again in a convincing manner. Faraway Lad had given me a top class feel that day and I felt that he was not short of being Champion Hurdle material. He has since been sold to America. The West Awake tried to do the Cheltenham/Liverpool double again, but with the Mildmay Course being so tight, it did not really suit horses wearing blinkers. He was knocked about a bit in the race and ended up finishing fourth, behind horses he had previously beaten on more galloping courses.

Border Burg, James Delahooke's hunter-chaser, who had won the Foxhunters over the big fences the previous year, was my ride in the big race. For some reason we didn't seem to click at Liverpool or, for that matter, on our previous outing at Newbury. Perhaps I should have had long legs like those of Alan Hill, the six feet four inch amateur, who had been so successful with him the previous season. Border Burg was very lethargic in the big race and we pulled up two out without really ever getting into the race at all.

The Whitbread at Sandown Park on 23rd April was Desert Orchid's next and final target for the season. A field of twelve were to line up, with both Desert Orchid and Kildimo having to give upwards of 20 lbs. to the field. It looked to be a virtually impossible task, reflected by the betting, with Aquilifer the 11 to 2 favourite, followed by Desert Orchid, Kildimo and Strands of Gold all on 6 to 1.

Not only was Desert Orchid giving away a bundle of weight, he was faced with a distance over which he had never won and the race tactics were crucial. The plan was to jump off and try to control the pace. It was a plan essentially based on optimism; in the same way that Desert Orchid couldn't win on a left-handed course, he had been labelled a front runner who could take a good hold. Then there was the question of whether he would stay in this company, as the previous year he had pulled up in the race due to problems with corns, and there had been concern this year prior to the race. Armed with such facts, it seemed inevitable that someone would take us on.

Having jumped the first in front, I got the impression the likes of Run and Skip and Memberson were frightened to challenge us for the lead. This suited our tactics well and for a complete circuit Desert Orchid coasted along in front jumping, as John Francome said, 'out of his stride'. He was not only giving me a wonderful feeling but also saving energy.

By this time, all the earlier scares about his corns had gone and at the second down the back I quickened the tempo. He lengthened his stride for one of his 'long leaps'. John Oaksey was heard to wince on the television but Tingle Creek at his best couldn't have jumped it better. No one took us on until the Railway fences for the final time, when Run and Skip took the lead from us. It didn't matter. By then we had created our own rhythm and to temporarily lose the lead was academic. Dessie was jumping like a buck, fast and accurately, and the only thing I had to be careful of was the extra-long one that he occasionally put in, making sure I wasn't left behind.

As we came to the Pond Fence, the third last, I knew we still had plenty left in the tank. Any thoughts of winning were still a long way off and my concern was the whereabouts of Kildimo, who comes with a late run. I wasn't kept in suspense for long - as we jumped the second last Kildimo loomed upsides us. It was the one sight I didn't want to see and the temptation was to suddenly get to work on Dessie, but that would have been the wrong thing to do; I had to remind myself to keep hold of his head and ask him for the extra gear I knew was there.

Coming to the last in a race like the Whitbread, with a challenger going equally well, is not an enviable situation to find oneself in. Meet it on a good stride and you are 'home and hosed' but what to do if your stride is wrong - kick or take a pull? Take a pull and you may throw the race away or kick and fall which would be a sacrilege. Not wanting to take any very positive action I let Dessie drift down the fence, giving him more room and bang, he was spot on.

Jumping the last I knew we would win, although the commentator on television wasn't so sure saying, 'We have a race on'. With head down, hands and heels and the benefit of some vocal encouragement he stormed up the Esher hill.

The reception as we returned to the winners enclosure was unbelievable, again prompting the commentator to remark, 'I have never, ever

The 1988 Gold Cup - Golden Friend leads Cavvies Clown and me; we finished second to Charter Party.

heard a crowd warm to a horse like they have to Desert Orchid'. Hats were thrown in the air and half the crowd must have rushed to the path back to the weighing room to try and given Dessie a congratulatory pat. One punter even ran up with a glass of champagne offering it to Janice, Dessie and myself despite the fact he'd backed Strands of Gold.

The cheer when I dismounted and got my customary kiss from Janice Coyle, who looks after Dessie - a kiss only guaranteed if we came back the winner, raised the roof. I weighed in and came out for my second Whitbread presentation.

The Queen Mother, an avid follower of jump racing, clearly knew something we didn't for, at the presentation, Her Majesty pointed out the orchid she was wearing.

All in all it was a good season - fifty-four winners including some very important races.

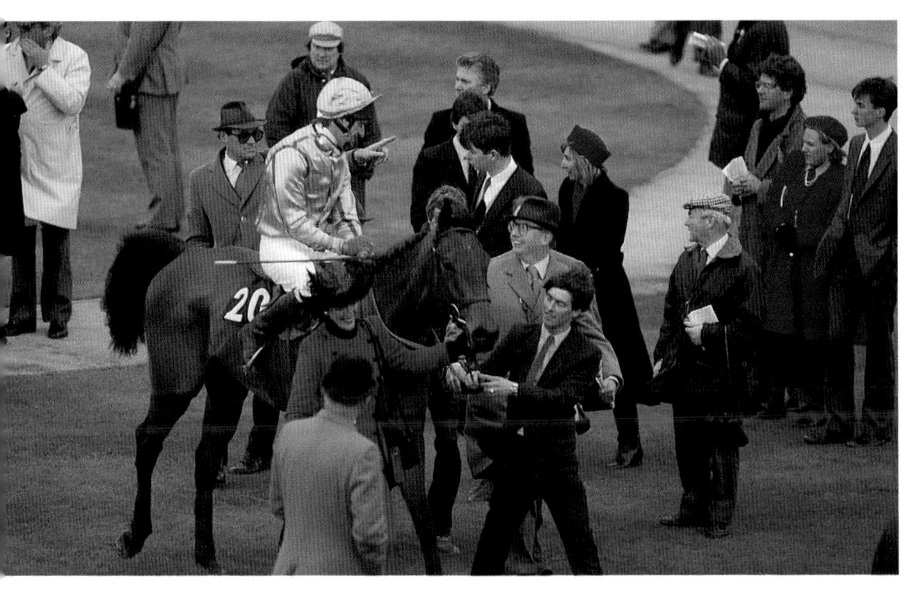

Christopher and Maggie Heath lead me in on Rebel Song, part of our 1988 Festival double.

The West Awake, the other Heath winner in our Festival double - both were trained by Oliver.

John Skull, the famous Swindon physiotherapist who patched me up and was especially brilliant when he got me back into the saddle for the 1988 Kempton Boxing Day meeting.

Fourth Season as Professional and Gold Cup
July 1988 - 1st May 1989

Kicking off a National Hunt season in the knowledge that you have such horses as Desert Orchid, Barnbrook Again, The West Awake, Rebel Song and Floyd to ride is a prospect anyone would relish.

I was once again re-united with John Jenkins for the 1988/89 season so, on top of Oliver's sixty horses, I had an additional forty of John's to ride. It is hardly surprising that people would come up to me and tell me how lucky I was; in my own mind I couldn't have agreed more. In fact, I wasn't thinking about how many winners I was going to ride, but the number of top races I was going to win. However, I had to play it down. I was fully aware that just one silly racing accident could alter everything. It was not worth provoking providence.

I don't know what I provoked, but I very nearly never started the season. Two days before the first meeting John Jenkins asked me to come up and school at his new establishment, at Royston, not far from Newmarket. The facilities there are excellent, with a modern yard and private gallops. Lucy decided to come and watch, something she had never done before and was never to do again. She had some extraordinary effect on John's youngsters and, from a previous record of one fall while schooling, I left Royston after that tortuous session having trebled the score, with a cracked rib and concussion to boot!

I didn't have my first win of the season until 10th September at Wincanton, a late start for me, but it was nothing to do with falls. The first of my stars to win a race was Floyd; he won at Kempton on 15th October carrying the top weight of 11 st. in the Ring and Brymer Hurdle. This was followed by another win on the 22nd October at Huntingdon. He was then sent up to Newcastle for the Fighting Fifth Hurdle in November. He is a real terrier of a horse who never knows when to give up, a true professional who could be compared with Billy Bremner. It was a tremendous race from two out and he won by half-a-length from the Mercy Rimmell trained Celtic Chief. The Fighting Fifth epitomized a fun day's racing - we all met at Mike Walsh's hotel near Ascot and, as one of Floyd's owners, he treated us to a superb breakfast before leaving for Heathrow to fly up to Newcastle. John Rumble, who is bald and red-faced and another owner/bookmaker, wore a very odd blue trilby and seemed far more concerned about his hat than Floyd that afternoon. So much so that Mike (who was quite rightly rather irritated by his fellow owner's concern for the hat at the expense of the horse) made him promise to trample ceremoniously on the hat on the winners' enclosure if Floyd won.

The hat suffered damage beyond repair. The victory ensured my mind was put at rest; David Elsworth, Floyd's trainer, had conjured up the idea of sending the little horse over fences. I had done my level best to dis-

Floyd (nearest camera) jumps the last in the Fighting Fifth Hurdle at Newcastle in November 1988, on the way to a hard fought win.

Dessie and I on the way to victory in the Tingle Creek Handicap at Sandown over two miles in December 1988.

suade him from this, thinking up a host of plausible reasons, including his history of bad legs. None of these dampened David's enthusiasm. As time wore on he became increasingly convinced that his idea was the answer and the Fighting Fifth was to be Floyd's last race over hurdles. At the same time I became ever more apprehensive but what I couldn't bring myself to do was to tell David that the thought of jumping fences on Floyd frightened the living daylights out of me. Luckily the Fighting Fifth brought about a reprieve for both of us.

I have as much respect for David Elsworth as a mixed trainer as anyone. His record in the past few years says it all. It doesn't matter if it's a two-year-old, a sprinter, a stayer, a hurdler, a Grand National horse or even Desert Orchid, he can train them. He has amazing judgement of a horse and however mad you might think an idea is, at the end of the day his judgement is nearly always vindicated.

There is a tremendous feeling of excitement to know that you have a guaranteed ride on not only the best, but also the most popular chaser in the country. With that in mind I felt it was only right to involve myself with the team associated with Desert Orchid and go down to Whitsbury, in the heart of Wiltshire, to ride the grey out before he ran. Rodney Boult, the head lad and regular partner of Dessie, and Janice Coyle, his ever smiling and devoted lad, played integral parts in his rise to fame and my appearance was more a token of appreciation.

As a jockey, riding out at a yard for the first time is a fairly exciting experience. The nerves tingle a bit; you know that the staff are watching your every move and you are being continually assessed. There is a danger of trying too hard. I arrived in my Audi Quattro wearing my 'best riding-out clothes', with well polished boots. There was something different about Whitsbury; I knew they were watching me as Rodney led me to Desert Orchid, giving me a list of instructions as to what buttons I could push and which ones to definitely avoid.

Such was the complexity of the instructions I felt like Nigel Mansell about to get into a new Ferrari, rather than Simon Sherwood climbing aboard Desert Orchid. The one big difference between Mansell's Ferrari and Desert Orchid is that the Ferrari has neither brains nor ears. Dessie listened, intrigued by the instructions. You don't become the most popular horse in this country for a decade without being a character. He knew that on the racecourse it was serious business but at home, in the privacy of the Whitsbury gallops, his standing in the yard would be further enhanced if he put his 'upstart' of a jockey in his place.

After two furlongs on the all-weather gallop, I don't think the pits team would have been too happy with Mansell had Dessie been a Ferrari. The revs were in the red and the speed off the clock. Salvation, for both my arms and my self respect, came in the form of a polo mint held out by David half way up the gallop. By then Dessie was satisfied that his little game had worked and from then on he was prepared to behave in a more reasonable manner!

'National stars' are never short of idiosyncrasies; Dessie is no exception and, like anyone with an air of importance, he feels his rightful place is at the head of the string. Woe betide any horse that comes upside him on the way home, playing with his bit and generally irritating him - back go his ears and the antagonist is quickly put in his place with a bump, not dissimilar to a 'ride-off' in polo.

Dessie going brilliantly at Kempton on Boxing Day.

Dessie's campaign for the season started at Wincanton, on 27th October in the Terry Biddlecombe Challenge Trophy over two miles and five furlongs. It was a conditions race ideally suited to Desert Orchid and while the opposition was good, none of them were up to his class. The racing public came in force and the crowd was twice the norm, with at least fifty at the start armed with cameras.

The plan was to get round and blow the cobwebs out but Dessie thought differently. He relished all the attention and put in a superb display of accurate jumping, if anything tending to show off. As we turned into the straight for the final time, the crowd started cheering. I allowed myself the benefit of a quick look over my shoulder and couldn't believe it when I saw we were twenty lengths clear. The exercise had been an unqualified success and all roads now led to Kempton Park on Boxing Day for the King George VI Chase.

The lack of suitable condition chases meant that occasionally Dessie had to be thrown-in at the deep end and give a mass of weight away in

A nice win at Ascot on 8th December 1988 in the The Daily Telegraph Hurdle on Calapaez.

Kempton on Boxing Day 1988 - Parading before the start on Dessie.

handicaps. The Tingle Creek Chase at Sandown Park on 3rd December was one such occasion, when he was set to give the enigmatic Vodkatini 24lbs. and Panto Prince 16lbs. in this prep race for Kempton. Conditions weren't ideal - the trip of two miles was on the sharp side, while the ground was a shade soft for him to be at his best. Fortunately, Vodkatini refused to race and Dessie came home a twelve-lengths winner in a common canter. The racing press went mad. This was the best performance in a handicap since Burrough Hill Lad in the 1984 Hennessy. The Cheltenham Gold Cup (a race never mentioned in the Burridge household) was mooted as a very real possibility, when it became increasingly evident there was no horse in the country which could live with Desert Orchid.

Four days later, at Huntingdon, I met with another setback which nearly put paid to the rest of the season. I had a nasty fall on Philip Mitchell's Guessing. Lucy showed total composure and behaved very bravely, helping me back to the car. I was sure it was nothing more than a groin strain but after an hour-and-a-half's sleep in the car on the way home, I woke up with a horrible, bloated feeling in my tummy. It was straight to the doctor where I fainted twice getting out of the car. He had no hesitation in sending me to Princess Margaret's Hospital in Swindon. I was suffering from internal bleeding and they estimated I had lost three or four pints of blood, something which meant nothing to me until I was told my body only holds nine pints! A couple of days and three transfusions later it dawned on me that I only had two weeks to get back in shape for the King George. It would certainly be a race against time.

It was virtually impossible to walk, my groin had seized up and I had bruising from my thighs to below the rib-cage. I dragged myself up and down the wards, pulling my drip along behind me. Life for a few days was very uncomfortable. Time passed far too quickly. Boxing Day was fast approaching but, thanks to John Skull, a physiotherapist in Swindon with plenty of experience of jump jockeys' needs, the route to recovery was greatly speeded up. My day entailed a visit to a health hydro pool, designed for paraplegics, many and various exercises and painful attempts to run. Four days before the King George a marked improvement was evident and two days later, I rode out for the first time. I wasn't very comfortable but felt good enough.

The Boxing Day meeting at Kempton Park has always been one of my favourites. There is a tremendously festive atmosphere and the enormous crowd seems genuinely interested in the racing. After quite a break, the sight of John Buckingham, Tom Buckingham and Andy Townsend (the valets in the weighing room) came as a great relief - I was really back and running. The valets gave me a cheerful and enthusiastic welcome back; they are wonderful companions in the changing room and extremely hard workers, arriving at the racecourse at about 8.00 a.m. and leaving two or three hours after racing.

Luckily I had a couple of rides before the King George, including a winner on Cruising Altitude, to put me in the right frame of mind for the big race. Once again, the big race went according to plan with the two of us being able to dictate the pace. I always found it best to let Dessie do his own thing for a couple of fences, which invariably meant going off too fast, but with a lot of shouting, telling him to steady up or, more frequently, to 'F....ing slow down!', he would soon steady to a more sensible pace. Once that initial buzz had gone I could relax. It didn't matter if another horse came upsides and took him on, he would take no notice.

Vodkatini, who had consented to race, improved to join me at the third last. For the first time I knew I was going to have to engage the turbo - we had jumped the fence a bit slowly, giving Kildimo the opportunity to get into the race. We all quickened approaching the second last, there was no quarter given and no room for the faint-hearted; it was imperative to ask for everything. We all met it well but Dessie was the quickest away and I then knew that as long as we jumped the last well we would win.

Dessie was in front of his most loyal crowd, he couldn't let them down and quickened into the final fence, hurdling it rather than jumping it. We were away and running and in the end won fairly easily. Having pushed the panic button the response had been instantaneous. He had, once and for all, proved that as a racehorse he was the complete article - he could lob along in front, ears pricked, jumping well but wasting no energy. Then at the business end, the ears would tell all: as they went back so the pace would quicken and the jumping flatten out, utilizing his energy to the maximum advantage. He was, quite simply, a natural.

Dessie and I coming in after our victory in the King George VI Chase, 1988.

Later in the season at Cheltenham - smiling faces everywhere after our Gold Cup victory.

Any previous doubts which a handful of the press had expressed as to Desert Orchid's ability to win a Gold Cup were now dispelled and the press, as a body, were united in their view that he had to run and win the Gold Cup. I had to agree with them. I couldn't see how he could be beaten, barring an accident. It might sound very arrogant, having never won a Gold Cup, but I hadn't been far away on Cavvies Clown, finishing second the year before and, no disrespect to Cavvies Clown, but Dessie gave me a totally different feel. Anyway, the formbook told the whole story - they had all taken him on and failed and the more I rode him, the less convinced I became about this supposed phobia to left-handed tracks.

David Elsworth knew the horse better than anyone. I'm not sure if he has ever received the credit he fully deserves for taking Desert Orchid to the top. The horse might have been a natural but it still takes a great deal of skill on the part of the trainer to keep a front runner interested and sound, without letting him fizz up. In this case that could so easily have happened, Desert Orchid being a very free-running type. David also sided with the press and felt Dessie should take his chance, but kept his opinions very much to himself.

Circumstances forced us to go back to two miles for the Victor Chandler Handicap Chase at Ascot on 14th January. It was a mark of Dessie's versatility that he could win a Whitbread over three miles and five furlongs one season, and then be contesting a top handicap over the minimum trip the next. But the fact of the matter was that over two miles he was not such a fun ride. He was inclined to rush his fences, putting in some foolhardy leaps, which neither helped his cause nor the nerves of his jockey.

The Panto Prince camp came up with a plan that was nearly to prove our undoing - to hassle us from the start. Going down the hill, the two horses matched stride for stride. Dessie jumped the ditch so big and long at the bottom of the hill, that he nearly stumbled and fell on landing. The race developed into a real fight from three out. Things didn't look good, Panto Prince was getting away from his fences quicker than we were; we were giving him over a stone and a half. I had to take the sort of action I had never dreamed of employing before - using my whip. I think Dessie and I were both equally horrified, but it had to be done. As we passed the winning post in front, I felt a great sigh of relief from Dessie, then his ears flicked forward as he regained his composure as if to say, 'well that was a bit close'.

While Desert Orchid was claiming all the media coverage, the potential 'young pretender', Barnbrook Again was keeping up his reputation. He had two wins and then the Arlington Series Final at Cheltenham on 28th January was the order of the day. The series was sponsored by Raymond Mould, so I was all the more keen to try and pick up this trophy. The top class field of four horses, all 'young pretenders', Rusch de Farges, potentially the best horse Peter Scudamore had ever ridden, Golden Freeze, from Jenny Pitman's all conquering yard and the enigmatic Private Views. It surprised me to find that Barnbrook Again was the third favourite at 5 to 2, considering his form was faultless and he was very much a class horse. Barnbrook Again won by three lengths from Rusch de Farges, but I felt that he was capable of better things. He jumped well and was always going to win but most of all I now felt that he would definitely get three miles.

All jockeys read the racing pages carefully and it is essential in a race to know who are the most likely horses to be involved in the finish. The forecast of betting gives an instant guide. Therefore jockeys are always talking about 2 to 1 favourites, 5 to 1 shots, etc., although betting doesn't play any part in the professional's life. In fact professionals aren't allowed to bet at all. History has proved that good jockeys need to be optimists and optimists aren't normally good gamblers. However, the same can't be said of stable lads, who are notorious for punting on their own charges.

By now Desert Orchid's participation in the Gold Cup seemed fairly certain and, with that in mind, it was decided to give him one more race before he had a tilt at steeplechasing's crown. The race in question was the Gainsborough Chase at Sandown at the beginning of February, where Desert Orchid had to give the fast improving Pegwell Bay, winner of both the Mackeson Gold Cup and the A.F. Budge Gold Cup, no less than 18 lbs..

For me, this was one of his most impressive victories. The race went according to plan. Pegwell took the lead going to the downhill fence, which allowed us a breather and time to prepare our attack. Jumping the last of the railway fences I had Pegwell Bay just in front of me and Desert Orchid felt very cosy underneath me. Coming to the Pond Fence, I thought we would win by three lengths going away. But at the last we lost a length on landing. We were going well enough not to push the panic button; hands and heels would suffice and Dessie responded well, winning comfortably by three-quarters of a length. In the end it was a pretty easy victory and I'm sure the winning distance was one of his little jokes with the Esher crowd, keeping them in suspense right to the line. His little joke backfired on me a bit as I became increasingly irritated by people trying to find fault with his performance.

Cheltenham looked full of exciting prospects - Cruising Altitude in the Waterford Supreme Novice Hurdle, Barnbrook Again in The Queen Mother Chase, Floyd in the Champion Hurdle and Desert Orchid in the Gold Cup. The two weeks before the famous meeting in March were going to be taken very calmly - there was no room for heroics. My sole concern was to get there in one piece.

Come Cheltenham or Liverpool, I am sure all jockeys will agree that their outlook on race-riding changes. During the weekday racing, such as Warwick or Plumpton, I had a tendency to be a bit too laid back in my approach to race-riding and at times was not ruthless enough, a fault that could irritate Oliver but then also benefitted certain horses. The

A victory kiss from Janice Coyle after the Victor Chandler Chase at Ascot, 14th January 1989.

Desert Orchid beats Pegwell Bay in the Racecall Gainsborough Chase, 14th February 1989. For me this was one of his most impressive wins.

Cheltenham Festival and Liverpool were the climax to the season and you never gave any room to anyone, whether it be Peter Scudamore or Steve Smith-Eccles. When riding, your vision as a jockey became totally blinkered and you only looked in front, never to your side or behind, to wonder whether you had hampered anyone. The speed was always greater but you had to conform to it, something Oliver had drummed into my head before my first ride at Cheltenham. These meetings really got you buzzing as a jockey.

Getting to Cheltenham is indeed a problem. Prestbury Park is not the most accessible place in the world and all credit to everyone for trying to improve the situation, but, at the end of the day, there is only one thing worse than a traffic jam and that is an organised traffic jam. Lambourn is about an hour from Cheltenham and, while a lot of people do the journey daily, I feel that one of the essential ingredients for a successful Cheltenham is to stay not far from the course.

With that in mind, I usually stayed with Nigel and Cathy Twiston-

Davies at Naunton, just outside Cheltenham. (Nigel breeds and races his own horses and is best remembered for that ultra game mare Mrs. Muck). With Peter and Maz Scudamore living two hundred yards away, there are few better places to stay to get the full atmosphere of 'The Festival'.

The atmosphere in the weighing room is unique; Cheltenham is the pinnacle of the season, a great deal is at stake and there is no margin for error. Reputations are made or shattered, fortunes won or lost. All the jockeys get 'big race fever', and instead of turning up to the racecourse an hour before racing, they all arrive two hours early. Consequently, a lot of time is spent reading the papers and whiling away the hours before the show starts. The banter has all been heard before - Steve Smith-Eccles complaining about his sore head, adding that he'll never drink whisky again (some chance!), Hywel Davies burbling on about some race he rode the day before, while rolling a cigarette, and Richard Rowe telling yet another appalling joke he heard on the way to the races.

The first day produced a third with Cruising Altitude and Floyd was a close fourth in the Champion Hurdle. Barnbrook Again won The Queen Mother Champion Two-Mile Chase on the second day. The first three fences in The Queen Mother Chase were run at a frightening speed; I have never jumped so fast. But it wasn't until we were coming down the hill that I truly felt that Barnbrook had the race at his mercy. That was until he took the third last fence by its roots; but Barnbrook was able to shrug off this mistake and win comfortably. This showed me the class of the horse; to be able to win a race of this calibre, having made such a costly mistake, added to the fact that I also genuinely felt that he did not really fire on the day. Certainly when we came into the unsaddling enclosure we got a very large cheer from his loyal band of Welsh supporters. Barnbrook Again's record at the National Hunt Festival in the last three years is really impressive - third in the Champion Hurdle, second in the Arkle Trophy and then his win this year in The Queen Mother Champion Chase.

But all these excitements slightly passed me by as the Gold Cup was my main thought throughout the meeting - it had been my main preoccupation for a very long time.

Nigel Twiston-Davies can, on occasions, suffer from something of a thirst and at the risk of arriving in the weighing room on Gold Cup day experiencing a similar complaint to Eccles, I was quite happy to share a couple of whiskies with him the night before. The justification was that it was purely medicinal and in the knowledge that Desert Orchid was well, the going perfect and the forecast of sun and wind ideal, I had no difficulty in falling asleep.

I was woken up at 6.30 a.m. the next morning by a sound that wasn't altogether encouraging. In fact; it was positively ominous. I thought I heard a car 'slushing' rather than driving past the window. I jumped out of bed and I promise you, if Eddie Fisher is a frightening person to see having caught you on a closed gallop, try me when I discover three inches of snow outside on Gold Cup day.

Most people came in for some sort of slating but the Meteorological Office definitely took the brunt of it; if Lucy was ever going to walk out on me this was the moment, as I stormed up and down behaving in the most extraordinary manner while everyone watched in amazement. Herbie was the first person (I regard him as a person) to grasp the situation and vanished very quickly until we got into the cars to go to the course.

Being something of an 'area weapon', Lucy drove me to the racecourse. As far as I was concerned the whole exercise was futile, racing couldn't possibly take place. The first person I saw was none other than Richard Burridge, with very wet feet. He had done nothing but walk the course all morning and told me that the fire-brigade were trying to take off the surface water. The whole situation became increasingly bizarre.

For the first time in the whole affair I thought of someone other than myself. Poor Richard. He had never been very keen on running in the Gold Cup and now this. Nothing in his life came before his beloved Desert Orchid; the horse's welfare was his primary concern. He knew the horse would hate the ground but if they did race, how could one man go against the entire racing world? As a script-writer he thought far more deeply than most and he was now confronted by a scenario he could so easily have thought up, lacking nothing in drama. The day before he had turned down a substantial offer for Desert Orchid, no doubt had had a sleepless night and now had wet feet from walking around a racecourse that his horse was supposed to hate, on ground he would loathe and the world and its wife was about to turn up hoping to witness a moment in racing history.

But all that was a long way off. The first question that had to be answered was whether racing would take place? Eventually the course was passed fit-to race. By then I had hoped racing would be cancelled and the Gold Cup re-scheduled for another day, as in the year Midnight Court won. Well, that wasn't going to happen and we all had to go through an agonizing period while Richard decided whether to run or not. In the end David Elsworth's calm, thoughtful reasoning won the day and the decision to run was taken.

Cantering to the start Desert Orchid lapped up the now customary cheer from the crowd. The ground was so soft he was getting through it fairly well but I was less than optimistic, worrying most about David's other runner, Cavvies Clown and Fulke Walwyn's very highly regarded Ten Plus. My feelings hardly improved when Dessie became slightly mulish at the start and planted a couple of times!

A roar from the crowd and we were off. The first circuit went according to plan, the pace was steady and Desert Orchid appeared to be enjoying himself. Jumping the first down the back for the first time the pace quickened with both Charter Party (winner of the Gold Cup the year before) and Ten Plus ranging upsides me. Dessie was jumping like a buck, enabling us to keep our position without having to quicken up much.

The battle up the hill with Yahoo starts in the Gold Cup.

Richard Dunwoody on Charter Party tried to squeeze me up coming to the second last ditch; reluctant as I was, I had to quicken up to hold our position. Coming down the hill I still felt happy but then we hit the fourth last hard. Luckily, we came out running and by the next we were back on the bridle. Kevin Mooney had been pushing Ten Plus along for sometime, but he still looked my main danger; tragically at the third last he fell and had to be destroyed. For an instant I thought the race was over and we would win.

It was only an instant, hardly had Ten Plus gone than a horse in yellow colours appeared next to me. For a moment I couldn't think who it was, then realised it was Tom Morgan on Yahoo. I couldn't bear it. I was going to be second again. Then, ten yards before the last, he changed legs and accelerated - I was back in with a chance.

From then on it was Desert Orchid's sheer guts and determination to win which got him up the famous hill. Jumping the last I felt physically knackered and can remember saying to myself, 'This is the Gold Cup, keep kicking.' So, head down and whip raised, I threw everything possible into it. I have never sat on a horse that showed such courage, by hook or by crook he was going to win and, almost as if to knock Yahoo out of the way, he hung left-handed, something no one would have thought possible, taking into account his previous history of drifting right-handed up the run-in.

Fifty yards from the line I knew we had won. It was a feeling I will never experience again. I thought the reception Dawn Run received after winning the Gold Cup could never be surpassed. How wrong I was. Janice was in flood of tears. I was virtually in tears and the whole crowd had gone mad. A type of mass hysteria seemed to overcome the place. People were almost trying to climb on Dessie who was loving every moment of it.

The walk from the racecourse to the winners' enclosure that day is an experience I am incapable of putting into words. I dare say Jonjo O'Neill on Dawn Run, or Bob Champion on Aldaniti in the Grand National, would be able to understand this feeling. Wherever I looked people were smiling and jumping up and down to get a glimpse of Desert Orchid. He seemed to enjoy it and as we entered the parade ring I can remember seeing a swarm of people and press running in our direction and I felt apprehensive. If ever Desert Orchid was going to call it a day, that was the moment, but not a bit of it. He pricked his ears, observed

Congratulations from the other jockeys after Dessie's and my win in the Gold Cup.

the situation and continued to walk on, well aware that he was the star. The cheer as he entered the enclosure was deafening. Everybody appeared to be applauding the horse who had won the top steeplechasing crown, in conditions totally adverse to him. I can remember seeing Martin Pipe, the trainer of Bonanza Boy, applauding the grey and even The Queen Mother seemed thrilled by the result.

Liverpool was our next objective although I confess my gut feeling was to give it a miss and pack up for the season. However I appreciated the need to go to Liverpool and Desert Orchid had apparently taken everything in his stride. As it turned out, Desert Orchid felt lethargic during the race and more prone to jumping right than normal. Peter Scudamore, on Beau Ranger, was trying to hassle us on the inside and I was aware that Yahoo would be biding his time ready to pounce near the end of the race. Going to the first fence down the back straight, the tempo quickened; four strides away I realised we were wrong but as always, sat still, expecting Dessie to put himself right with a shuffle of

Her Majesty The Queen Mother presents me with a trophy after the Gold Cup.

Desert Orchid is led in unharmed at Liverpool by Richard Burridge after our fall in 1989. I got a lift back in the ambulance with Richard Dunwoody who had fallen, independently at the same fence, on Charter Party.

his ever-agile feet. But there was only an apathetic reaction. Dessie hit the top of the fence hard, but not very hard and crumbled on landing. It was the type of jumping mistake that he normally made little of and kept galloping. Instead it was as if a tired horse had given in but luckily the pair of us got up unharmed. It was a shock and I was sad in the knowledge that it would almost certainly be the last time I sat on Dessie in a race.

The remainder of the Liverpool meeting picked up. I was second in the next race and on the second day I won on Villierstown in the John Hughes Memorial Chase over the National Course. Villierstown, owned by Mr. P. Pillar and trained by W.A. (Arthur) Stephenson, although small in stature, was the ride of a lifetime. It was always one of my ambitions to win a race over the big fences and it could not have been achieved in a more thrilling way. Villierstown only made one mistake at the fourth last, probably due to my over-excitement, but he managed to jump the fence, although I must have seriously hampered him. Furthermore I

Presentations from Mrs. John Hughes after I'd won the first running of the John Hughes Memorial Chase on Villierstown at Liverpool. To the left the new Clerk of the Course, John Perrett.

was particularly thrilled to win the first running of this Memorial Race as John Hughes, who did so much to save the National, was loved by everybody in the racing world.

In the National, I rode The Thinker, the top-rated horse, carrying 11 st. 10 lbs., priced at 10 to 1 third favourite and again trained by that master, Arthur Stephenson, a gentleman I always enjoyed riding for. It is always easy to be wise after the event and as we jumped Becher's for the second time, I was quite content, but a hiccough on landing appeared to take the stuffing out of The Thinker and my immediate reaction was to let the horse recover his wind, which cost me ten lengths and, at that stage of the race, it was too much. We ended up third, getting beaten seven lengths by Little Polvier and I questioned myself for a long time after as to whether I should have kicked on, having made that mistake. If I had, I may have won the great race.

A journey to Ayr with Oliver, John Francome, Arthur Boyd-Rochfort (the owner) and myself had all the potential ingredients for having a laugh. Aldino was to run in the Scottish Champion Hurdle on 14th April. We all met up at Heathrow and took the shuttle to Glasgow. Arthur, 'The Captain's' only son (i.e. the late Captain Sir Arthur Boyd-Rochfort - The Queen's Trainer) and a half-brother of Henry Cecil, is always game for a laugh, but I don't think he had bargained for John Francome's antics. We hired a car at the airport and, foreseeing trouble ahead, Oliver and myself hopped in the back, while John took the wheel, leaving Arthur with no option but to take the front passenger seat, quickly fastening his seat belt. A lot of revving-up went on in the car-park and the Fiesta 1.1L appeared to get quite excited as John quipped, 'Don't worry Arthur. I've settled down a lot now.' A false sense of security shone across Arthur's face as John revved the car to the maximum, fired it off in the direction of the exit and slammed on the handbrake, causing a 360 degree turn.

'Just trying the car out to see if it is safe', said John. Arthur appeared somewhat concerned and laughed nervously. We left the airport and, as we approached the motorway from the slip road, the car suddenly took a lurch up the bank, assisted by the driver, as if to take a short-cut onto the motorway and then back down again.

'Just seeing how the car handles grass', commented John. Arthur had had enough and told John to 'behave', which of course made him worse. We arrived in Ayr somehow, whereupon Aldino won the Scottish Champion Hurdle with top weight.

The Thinker, in the centre with orange and green colours, hiccoughs at Becher's second time in the 1989 Seagram Grand National. It may have cost us the race.

My last ride, winning on Knighton Lad, 1st May 1989 at Haydock.

My last ride in public was at Haydock on lst May 1989 on Knighton Lad, owned by Mr. and Mrs. South and trained by Oliver. I had not decided prior to the race that I would definitely 'hang up my boots' but I felt that if we won perhaps I should. The horse did win and I can remember pulling up and saying to Peter Scudamore 'shall I call it a day?'. Peter knew I was going to pack up that season and thought it was a good time to do so. When I dismounted I told Oliver that was it, he patted me on the back and, as it was obvious something was going on, the press were soon round asking what it was all about.

It was the end of my riding career. I was soon inside the weighing room cracking a couple of bottles of champagne with my ex-colleagues.

New Careers
2nd May 1989 -

I had had a good run for my money and Tim Cox, who has kindly done some statistical work on my record, tells me that I have had 1662 rides since the 1981/1982 season when I rode my first winner under Rules propor. Sixty-eight winners came in my last season. I won 345 races which is a strike rate of nearly 21% and probably justified my attitude in not accepting rides other than for stables for which I normally rode.

A well known comment in racing says, 'the racing business is fine, if only there weren't the owners'. During my stint riding it was one paradox which never affected me, as in general I was lucky enough to ride for some of the best owners.

I genuinely sympathise with the lot of owners who have to suffer the classic racing syndrome whereby they buy a horse for a large amount of money and it proves to be rather backward and needs time. This costs the owner extra money and a lot of patience. Unfortunately for both sides it is very frustrating but hopefully beneficial in the long run.

The late David Bott of R.E.A. Bott (Wigmore Street) Ltd. showed fantastic concern when The Breener, his potential star, was destroyed at Cheltenham. That night he turned up at Oliver's yard at Rhonehurst unannounced. As we sat there feeling sorry for ourselves, he grabbed hold of the situation by the scruff of the neck, took us all out to dinner and two hours later he had bought an equally exciting horse on the telephone from Ireland, Drive on Jimmy.

I was even treated to a kiss on each cheek every time I rode a horse for Mrs. Christopher Heath, a custom that probably caused a few raised eyebrows in the paddock, but for us it was a good luck ritual which generally worked - perks of the retainer!

Sadly, in racing, the owners have to subsidise a lot of the racing structure. That is to say that unfortunately not enough money is ploughed back into racing, causing a serious deficit at the grass roots. Stable lads, who earn an agricultural wage of around £100 a week before tax and other deductions, simply cannot afford to buy a house, as their wage doesn't begin to cover a mortgage. Therefore good lads end up drifting away from the racing business and into factories, where they can earn a comparatively good income. The trainers are not to blame as their training bills generally cover a break even point, but leave nothing extra for re-investment or improvement, or the ability to increase the lads' wages. The only exception to this may be the very best flat race yards.

The owners cannot continually be expected to pay ever-increasing training bills, unless there is a major increase in prize money. If prize money was brought into line with say France or Australia, the whole situation would improve. The bookmakers' contribution to racing is minimal in this country compared to what their equivalents in France and Australia have to plough back into the sport. More money from the bookmakers would mean more money for the whole racing industry, especially National Hunt racing. It would all become much healthier and, most importantly, the money would filter right down to the grass roots. The situation over the lads' wages is very worrying for a potential trainer such as myself. I know what it is like to live on racing wages and I wasn't married when I started at Newmarket with Tom Jones.

The same applies for National Hunt jockeys. For an average National Hunt jockey getting 200 rides a year with fifteen winners, his income is approximately £15,000 per annum. His main overheads are travelling expenses, which are in the region of £5,000 a year, leaving him with a meagre £10,000 a year before tax and valet fees. A paltry income for a high risk job. I was lucky as I had such wonderful horses to ride and therefore was making a well above average income, but I am talking here about the 'average' jockey who didn't have my lucky breaks.

When thoughts of retirement start going through your mind, the reality should be seriously thought over. Having progressed from amateur to professional I always thought I would ride for two years. I had started point-to-pointing back in 1978 so I had been in the game, in one way or another, for quite a long time before turning pro. To have done

'My mate', Herbie, specially photographed by Fiona Vigors for the book in early September 1989.

four seasons was double what I had envisaged, but then I didn't anticipate enjoying myself so much, or being associated with such good horses. With the likes of Desert Orchid, Barnbrook Again, The West Awake, Floyd and Cruising Altitude waiting on the sidelines for another season some people must consider me mentally deranged to have called it a day.

Soon after Cheltenham I had come to terms with the possibility of giving up race-riding. To have won a Gold Cup, two Whitbreads, two King George's, a Queen Mother Champion Two-Mile Chase, five other Festival winners and a number of races at the Grand National meeting in such a short time was a far greater achievement than I could have ever imagined when I turned professional. I was still in one piece, still walking sound and still, arguably, the full biscuit. So I felt why not pull out while the going is good, rather than carrying on, possibly for one season too many, and regretting it.

My long term plans are to train and we, Lucy and myself, are facing the exciting challenge of building a racing stable from scratch at East Ilsley. This is a few miles further down the valley from where we now live. The facilities are excellent and I will have my own all-weather gallop, access onto grass and schooling grounds. We have a number of nice young horses out at grass, so come July 1990 we should be ready to go. This new career would not have been possible without the support of many people, especially my parents. I am determined to succeed in my new profession and feel quietly confident about the future.

Since retiring I have written this book which, with the proof-reading and corrections has kept me fairly busy during the months of June to September this year and in November I start as a commentator for S.I.S. Television. Also, by the time you read this, Lucy and I will be married - the wedding was on 29th September, 1989.

As for Desert Orchid the memories I have of race-riding primarily revolve around him. To me and, I expect, to quite a few of his avid followers, he is much more than just a brilliant racehorse. He is fortunate in having a God-given gift - charisma, something which is very rare. Undoubtedly he is one of the four most popular chasers to run this century and can only really be compared with Golden Miller, Arkle and Red Rum, when it comes to popular appeal.

To have been associated with Dessie is a privilege and he enabled me to reach far greater heights as a jockey than would otherwise have been possible. All nine victories remain at the top of my recollections and although we blotted our copybook in the last race, we at least achieved 'Nine out of Ten'.

Lucy and I at Ham playing polo in a celebrity charity match in aid of the Bob Champion Cancer Fund, September 1989.

Simon Sherwood's

Editor's Note

Selling Races are races run on the flat, over hurdles and over fences where the winner is sold by public auction after the race. The main aim of these races is to give moderate horses the chance to win although in the past they have been used in gambling coups. The conditions are framed to try and stop good/valuable horses entering as the fixed selling price of the winner is low and only gives the winning owner 20% of proceeds over that price.

An example might be winner £1,600 prize money + horse to be sold for £2,000. If the horse was sold for £2,000 the owner would get £1,600 prize money + £2,000 for the horse, a total of £3,600. The owner loses his horse. But if the same owner 'buys back' his horse for £5,000, the finances would be £1,600 prize money, £2,000 'selling price' plus 20% of 'surplus' over £2,000 i.e. £600, making a total of £4,200. The owner pays £5,000 to retain his horse making a loss of £800. The balance of the surplus, 80%, or in this case £2,400 goes to the racecourse.

Riding Record

My record under National Hunt Rules since 1981/82 when I rode my first winner.

	1st	2nd	3rd	Unpl.	Mounts	Win %
1981/82	9	2	1	5	17	52.9%
1982/83	13	11	4	44	72	18.1%
1983/84	28	7	13	62	110	25.5%
1984/85	30	22	17	98	167	18.0%
1985/86	79	50	53	181	363	21.8%
1986/87	64	45	37	140	286	22.4%
1987/88	54	51	41	184	330	16.4%
1988/89	68	42	41	166	317	21.5%
	345	230	207	880	1662	20.8%

The first four seasons I was an amateur and the last four a professional.

I also rode five winners on the flat as an amateur and a winner in Sweden; the above record does not include 'point-to-points'.

My ten rides on Desert Orchid.

1 Kempton King George VI Rank Chase 26 December 1986

1) Desert Orchid, 7 years–S. Sherwood, 11st. 10lbs.
2) Door Latch, 8 years–R. Rowe, 11st. 10lbs.
Distance: 15 lengths

2 Liverpool Chivas Regal Cup 7th April 1988

1) Desert Orchid, 9 years–S. Sherwood, 11st. 5lbs.
2) Kildimo, 8 years–G. Bradley, 11st. 5lbs.
Distance: 8 lengths

Simon Sherwood's

My ten rides on Desert Orchid *(continued)*

3 Sandown Whitbread Gold Cup 23rd April 1988
1) Desert Orchid, 9 years–S. Sherwood, 11st. 11lbs.
2) Kildimo, 8 years–J. Frost, 11st. 12lbs.
Distance: 2½ lengths

4 Wincanton Terry Biddlecombe Challenge Trophy 27th October 1988
1) Desert Orchid, 9 years–S. Sherwood, 11st. 8lbs.
2) Bishops Yarn, 9 years–R. Guest, 11st. 8lbs.
Distance: 15 lengths

5 Sandown Tingle Creek Handicap Chase 3rd December 1988
1) Desert Orchid, 9 years–S. Sherwood, 12st. 0lbs.
2) Jim Thorpe, 7 years–M. Dwyer, 10st. 8lbs.
Distance: 12 lengths

6 Kempton King George VI Rank Chase 26th December 1988
1) Desert Orchid, 9 years–S. Sherwood, 11st. 10lbs.
2) Kildimo, 8 years–J. Frost, 11st. 10lbs.
Distance: 4 lengths

7 Ascot Victor Chandler Handicap Chase 14th January 1989
1) Desert Orchid, 10 years–S. Sherwood, 12st. 0lbs.
2) Panto Prince, 8 years–B. Powell, 10st. 6lbs.
Distance: head

8 Sandown Racecall Gainsborough Handicap Chase 4th February 1989
1) Desert Orchid, 10 years–S. Sherwood, 12st. 0lbs.
2) Pegwell Bay, 8 years–C. Llewellyn, 10st. 10lbs.
Distance: ¾ length

9 Cheltenham Tote Gold Cup 16th March 1989
1) Desert Orchid, 10 years–S. Sherwood, 12st. 0lbs.
2) Yahoo, 8 years–T. Morgan, 12st. 0lbs.
Distance: 1½ lengths

10 Liverpool Martell Cup Chase 6th April 1989
1) Yahoo, 8 years–T. Morgan, 11st. 5lbs.
2) Delius, 11 years–B. Dowling, 11st. 5lbs.
Fell–Desert Orchid, 10 years–S. Sherwood, 11st. 13lbs.